I Can Draw
Cartoons

A step-by-step guide to drawing fantastic cartoons

Paul B. Davies • Kevin Faerber
Terry Longhurst • David Pattison

Text by Amanda O'Neill

p

This is a Parragon Publishing Book
First published in 2002

Copyright © Parragon 2002

Parragon Publishing
Queen Street House
4 Queen Street
Bath BA1 1HE, UK

Designed, produced, and packaged by
Stonecastle Graphics Limited

Designed by Paul Turner and Sue Pressley
Edited by Philip de Ste. Croix

All rights reserved. No part of this publication may be
reproduced, stored in a retrieval system, or
transmitted in any way or by any means, electronic,
mechanical, photocopying, recording, or otherwise,
without the prior permission of the copyright holder.

ISBN 0-75258-723-4

Printed in U.A.E.

About This Book

Cartoons are drawings which take a humorous look at the world. They are fun to look at, and they are fun to draw. This book shows you how to create a host of entertaining characters, building up your drawings in easy stages.

The tools you need are simple — paper, a selection of pencils, and an eraser. Fairly thick paper is best to work with (very thin paper wears through if you have to rub out a line).

To color in your drawings, you can use paints, crayons, colored inks, or felt-tip pens. Fine felt-tips are useful for drawing outlines, while thick ones are better for coloring in.

Remember that cartoons aren't meant to be realistic. They are imaginative and exaggerated. You can draw monsters or fairies, create cute animals or fearsome dinosaurs, or even give a cartoon character a nose that is bigger than his feet. Anything is possible in cartoon-land.

But they are meant to be recognizable. You need to get inside your subject just as much as if you were making an accurate portrait. Most cartoons take some feature of the subject and exaggerate it to comic effect. So you need to decide which feature you want to emphasize. It may be the way your subject stands, or moves. It may be big feet or a funny expression.

The step-by-step drawings in this book will give you plenty of ideas to get you started. After that, there's a whole world out there to draw!

Happy Fish

Fish come in many different shapes — long and thin, like eels, or short and rounded. But their bodies are always made up of curves. By exaggerating these natural curves, you can make your fish comically fat and cheerful-looking.

Start with a simple circle for the body.

Draw a triangle at one end, marking out the position of the tail.

Add an upright fin on the back.

Now draw two little circles, placed high up, for goggling eyes.

The two lower fins are formed by smaller, more rounded shapes than the back fin. They don't need to look realistic — in fact, they might suggest feet!

Sketch in a big happy smile. It curves beyond the edge of your circle to form a bulging lower lip. At the inside edge of the mouth, a small crescent shape forms a smiley dimple.

Now you can start inking in your details. Draw the tail within its guideline triangle, and shape the other fins with curvy lines.

You don't need to draw in all the scales — but you can suggest them with a few bold wavy lines. A line of bubbles gives a fun effect.

A little shading on the fins, tail and scales adds the final touch. Show your finished drawing to your friends, and they'll think you're fishing for compliments!

Sleepy Cat

Cats take sleeping very seriously. They invented the catnap, and spend two-thirds of their lives practicing it. When awake, cats have long, elegant, flowing lines — but a sleepy cat curls itself into a short, round shape like a fur hat.

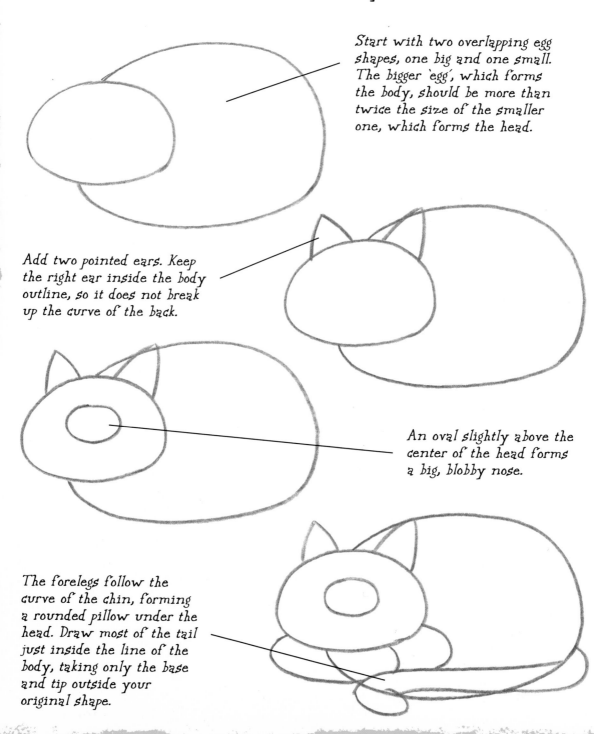

Start with two overlapping egg shapes, one big and one small. The bigger 'egg', which forms the body, should be more than twice the size of the smaller one, which forms the head.

Add two pointed ears. Keep the right ear inside the body outline, so it does not break up the curve of the back.

An oval slightly above the center of the head forms a big, blobby nose.

The forelegs follow the curve of the chin, forming a rounded pillow under the head. Draw most of the tail just inside the line of the body, taking only the base and tip outside your original shape.

Two simple curves create a pair of eyes closed in sleep. When you draw in the hind leg, use a generous sweeping line so that the leg takes up about half the body space.

To finish the face, draw in big fat cheeks curving from just below the top of the nose. Make the outer edges jagged, to suggest fur, and add little dots for the whisker roots.

Ink in your lines, and add bold coat markings. Real cats have complicated fur patterns, but cartoon cats look better if you simplify these into a regular, eye-catching design.

The whole drawing is made up of curves, giving a rounded, comfortable effect. Paws folded into a pillow under his chin, the sleepy cat is a picture of comfort — snug and smug.

Big-Ears the Elephant

From Babar to Dumbo, not forgetting Hathi in *The Jungle Book*, cartoonists have loved elephants. You may also be inspired by early Western pictures of elephants by artists who had never seen one, but only heard descriptions.

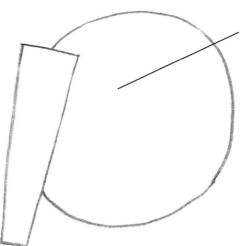

Start with these two shapes — a rough circle for the huge body, and a long, four-sided shape for the head and trunk.

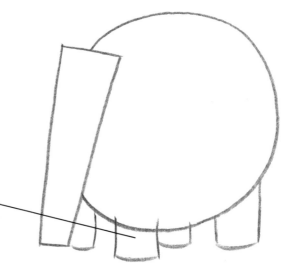

Draw four short, thick legs. By making them much shorter than in real life, you make the body look even bigger.

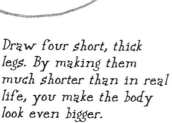

Draw two large arch-shaped ears, reaching from the top of the head to halfway down.

Add round eyes, about a third of the way down the head, and a simple tusk just below the ear.

A couple of raised eyebrows create a surprised expression. Don't forget to add a tail at the other end.

What is green and has a trunk? An elephant that's been picked too soon.

Ink in your outlines, curving the legs slightly inward to make the feet look bigger.

Now you can shape the head, rounding the forehead and making the trunk bulge, then taper. Make the lower edges of the ears rough and floppy.

Use light and dark shading to make your elephant look really solid. The dark shadow on the ground gives a great impression of size and weight

What do you get if you cross an elephant with peanut butter?

A spread that never forgets!

Smiley Snail

As most people know, a snail is only a slug with a mobile home! Most people find slugs rather unlovable, but the addition of a shell gives the snail a certain charm — unless you're a gardener. It also makes him more interesting to draw than his slimy cousin.

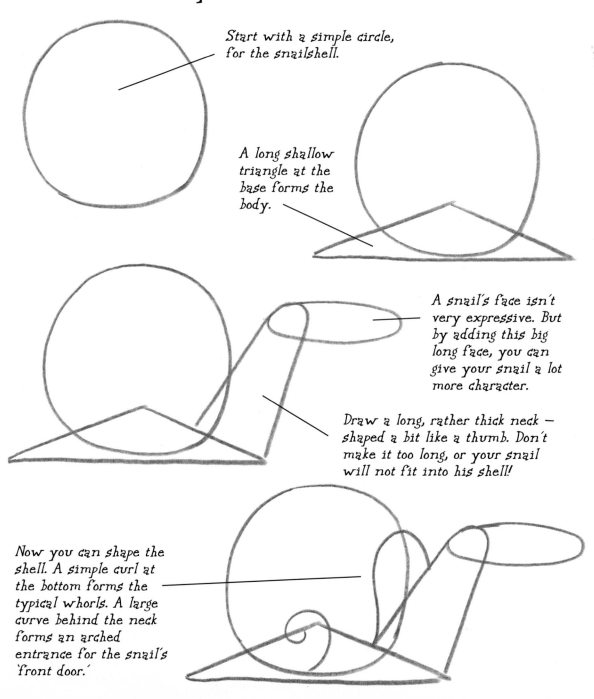

Start with a simple circle, for the snailshell.

A long shallow triangle at the base forms the body.

A snail's face isn't very expressive. But by adding this big long face, you can give your snail a lot more character.

Draw a long, rather thick neck — shaped a bit like a thumb. Don't make it too long, or your snail will not fit into his shell!

Now you can shape the shell. A simple curl at the bottom forms the typical whorls. A large curve behind the neck forms an arched entrance for the snail's 'front door.'

Draw the eyes on stalks at the top of the head. Make the stalks curve forward, so that the snail is actually looking in the direction he faces.

Add an inner curve to the 'door' of the shell, to form a rim (or 'door frame').

A series of gently curving stripes gives shape to the shell. Now you can finish off the head, with a smiley mouth and a pair of eyebrows — which float in space above the eyes.

Finish inking in your outlines, drawing a border to the lower edge of the snail's body to make it look more solid. A clump of grass will provide your snail with something to eat!

What kind of snail lives in Sherwood Forest?

Alan-a-Snail!

Lofty the Giraffe

The giraffe is a walking watchtower! His great height helps him see for miles across the savannah, so no enemy can sneak up on him.

Draw a long, flattened oval for the head.

Now draw a big blobby nose on top of the head, at the end.

This long spike forms the neck. Extend it across the head and just beyond. The point at the top will show you where to put the eyes!

These two little circles will form the knobs on the end of the horns. Start a little way inward from the back of the head.

Using the point of the neck 'spike' as a guide, draw two eyes perched on top of the head. Behind them, draw the horns.

Now add two long ears, shaped like leaves and laid flat on either side of the eyes.

Shape the neck where it joins the head, and hollow out the underside of the jaw. A tufty fringe round the eyes gives character to the head.

Draw in the bristly mane, and spots, and give your giraffe a leaf to munch.

That long neck makes a great periscope — but imagine being a giraffe with a sore throat!

Honey Bear

Bears love honey. In the wild, they have to rob bees' nests to get it, and usually get well stung in the process. For cartoon bears, life is easier because honey comes in jars. All this bear has to worry about is finding a comfortable place to enjoy his feast!

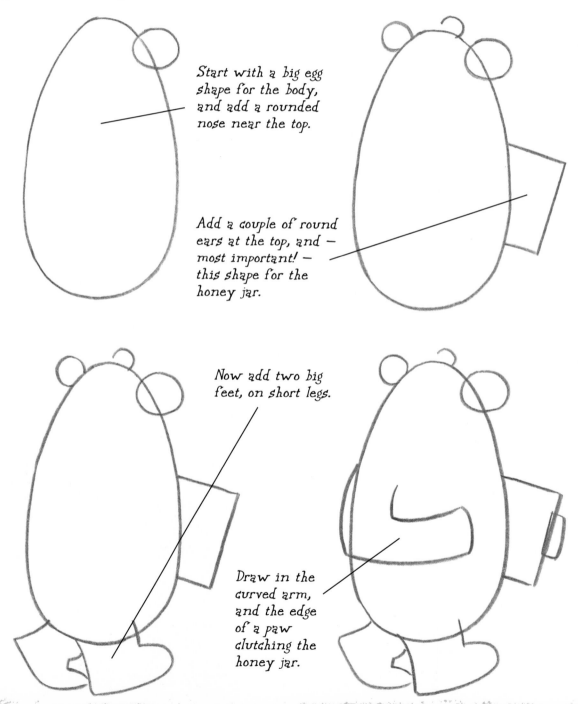

Start with a big egg shape for the body, and add a rounded nose near the top.

Add a couple of round ears at the top, and — most important! — this shape for the honey jar.

Now add two big feet, on short legs.

Draw in the curved arm, and the edge of a paw clutching the honey jar.

Two small round eyes go just at the top of the head.

Now you can put in the facial features. The little tongue peeps out of the mouth in anticipation.

Finish your outline, and label the honey jar with a picture of a bee. Add a shiny highlight to the big, black nose.

What do Baloo the Bear and Winnie the Pooh have in common?

Their middle names!

Chunky Chicken

Chickens are comical figures even in real life. Their chunky bodies balance between ridiculously small heads and legs. They are the busybodies of the farmyard, bustling about importantly and peering around with little bright eyes.

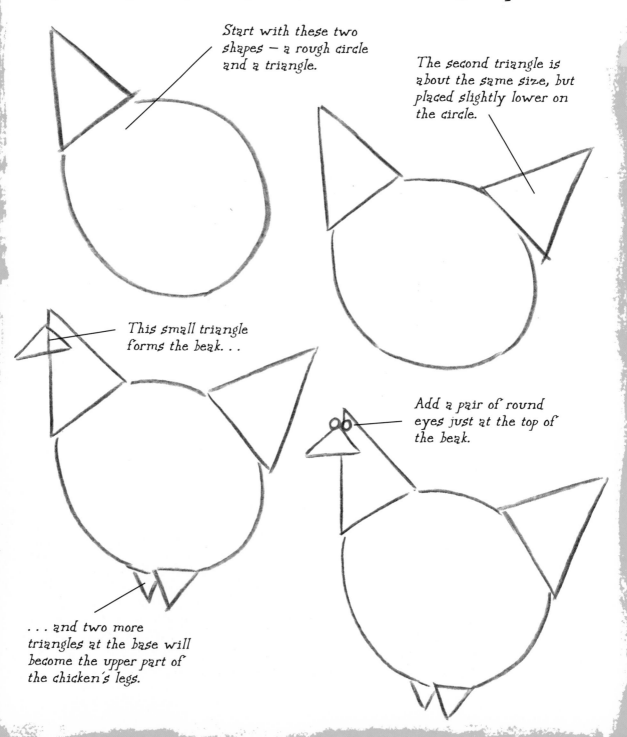

Start with these two shapes — a rough circle and a triangle.

The second triangle is about the same size, but placed slightly lower on the circle.

This small triangle forms the beak. . .

Add a pair of round eyes just at the top of the beak.

. . . and two more triangles at the base will become the upper part of the chicken's legs.

Draw a comb on top of the head, and two small wattles under the beak.

Add pupils to the eyes, draw in a wing and shape the tail feathers. Give a gentle curve to the neck and tail to form the ends of the dumpy, boat-shaped body.

Ink in your outlines and sketch in a few feathers on the wing and breast.

Now you can add the lower legs and long, flat feet.

Everyone knows the joke, 'Why did the chicken cross the road?' But do you know what to call a person who tells chicken jokes?

A comedihen!

Spike the Hedgehog

When is a hog not a hog? When it's a hedgehog! The only piggy thing about this little ball of spikes is the way he snorts and snuffles over his food. With a hundred spines per square inch, he is one of the prickliest characters you will ever meet.

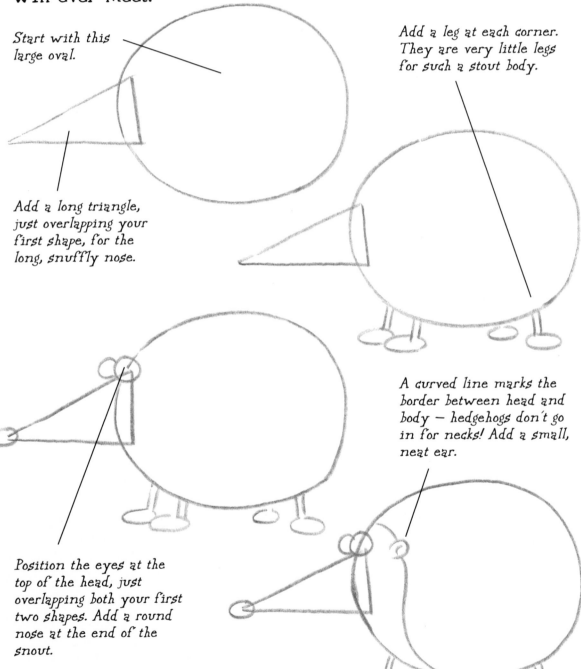

Start with this large oval.

Add a long triangle, just overlapping your first shape, for the long, snuffly nose.

Add a leg at each corner. They are very little legs for such a stout body.

A curved line marks the border between head and body — hedgehogs don't go in for necks! Add a small, neat ear.

Position the eyes at the top of the head, just overlapping both your first two shapes. Add a round nose at the end of the snout.

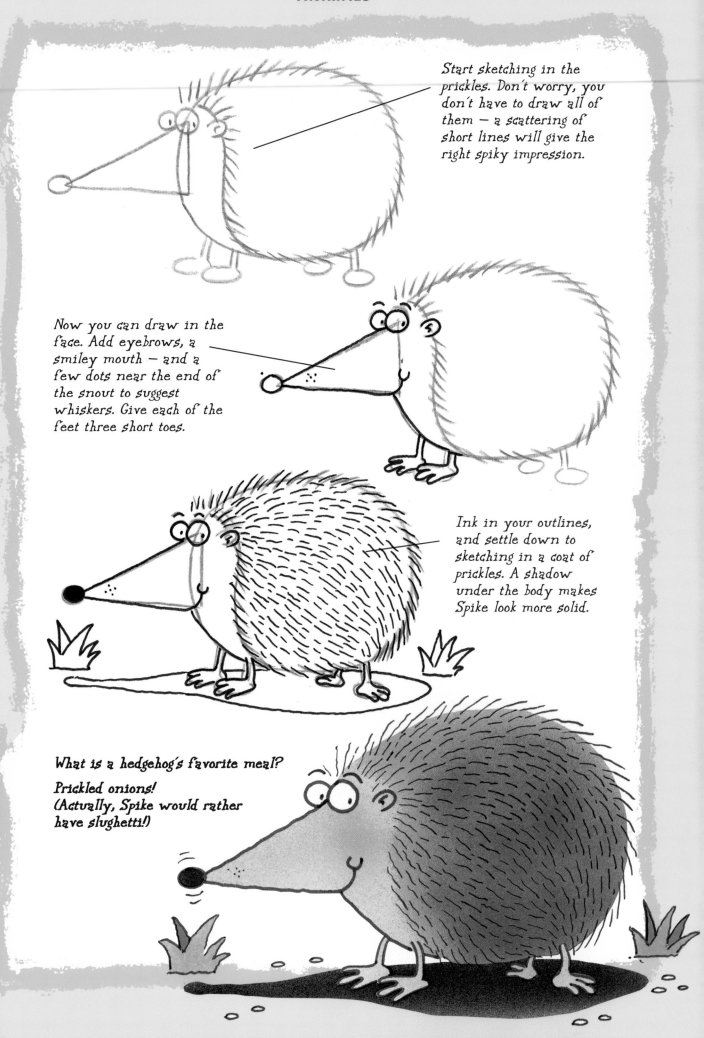

Start sketching in the prickles. Don't worry, you don't have to draw all of them — a scattering of short lines will give the right spiky impression.

Now you can draw in the face. Add eyebrows, a smiley mouth — and a few dots near the end of the snout to suggest whiskers. Give each of the feet three short toes.

Ink in your outlines, and settle down to sketching in a coat of prickles. A shadow under the body makes Spike look more solid.

What is a hedgehog's favorite meal?

Prickled onions!
(Actually, Spike would rather have slughetti!)

Porky Pig

Our view of pigs is strange. We are often rather rude about them — 'dirty pigs' and 'greedy swine.' Yet, at the same time, we find their comfortable round shape rather appealing, so we enjoy toy pigs, cartoon pigs — and, of course, piggy banks.

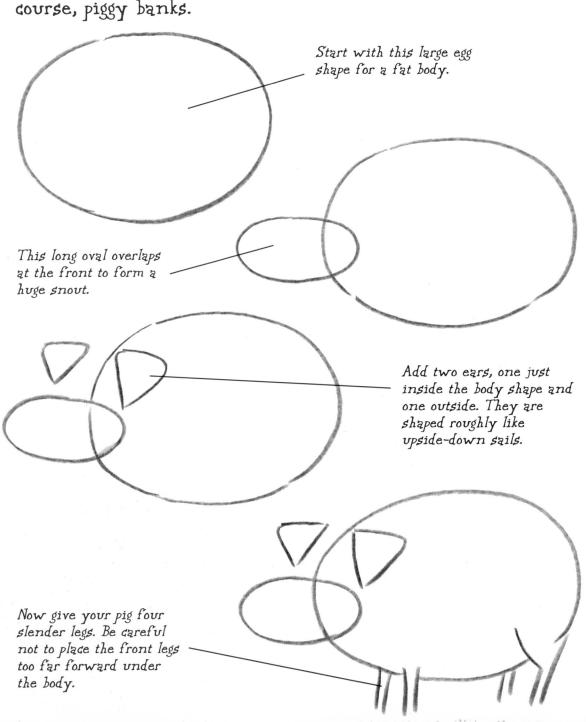

Start with this large egg shape for a fat body.

This long oval overlaps at the front to form a huge snout.

Add two ears, one just inside the body shape and one outside. They are shaped roughly like upside-down sails.

Now give your pig four slender legs. Be careful not to place the front legs too far forward under the body.

Fill in the face around the snout and ears. Add a gentle curve stretching from in front of the forelegs to beneath the snout, to form the chest and neck.

Finish the head with two little piggy eyes and a couple of wide-spaced nostrils. They make Porky look vaguely surprised

Pigs like their comfort, so draw in a shelter.

Why don't piglets ever listen to their father?

Because they find him such a boar!

You can color your pig pink, or banded, or spotted, depending on your taste. A dappling of spots helps to make him look more solidly rounded.

Cool Camel

The 'ship of the desert' is famous for two things. One is its 'backpack,' the hump in which it keeps emergency supplies for desert life. The other is its sneer. Few people can sneer half as well as a camel — our mouths aren't made for it.

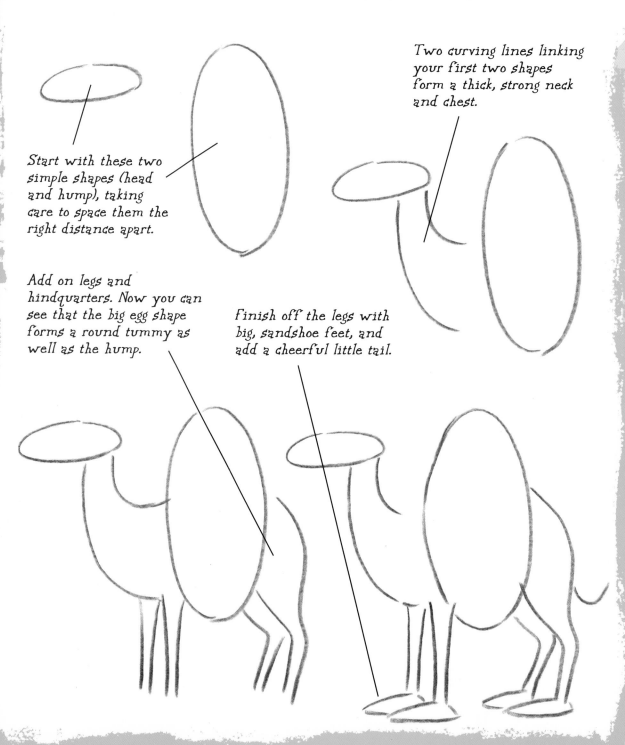

Start with these two simple shapes (head and hump), taking care to space them the right distance apart.

Two curving lines linking your first two shapes form a thick, strong neck and chest.

Add on legs and hindquarters. Now you can see that the big egg shape forms a round tummy as well as the hump.

Finish off the legs with big, sandshoe feet, and add a cheerful little tail.

Top off the head with eyes, a rounded forehead, and an ear. Sketch in knobbly knees.

Crown the hump with a jagged-edged topping to represent shaggy hair.

Ink in the outlines, bringing out the curves a little more. Add a sticking plaster to our poor, tired old friend.

A little pyramid in the background will help to make your camel feel at home.

Hungry Mouse

Mice are among the most popular of cartoon characters. Mickey Mouse, Speedy Gonzales, Dangermouse, Topo Gigio, and Jerry (of Tom and Jerry fame) are just a few mouse favorites.

Add a pair of great big feet, a second ear — and a large square of cheese.

Start with these three shapes — rather like a bunch of balloons.

The eyes and nose are simple blobs drawn on to the head.

Add a bulge at the back to make a fat bottom. The final shape of the body will be more pear-shaped than oval. Don't forget the tail!

Draw in the arms and simple hands. One hand, naturally, reaches toward that tempting lump of cheese.

It's a dark night, and you can't get to sleep because you can hear a mouse squeaking in your bedroom. What should you do?

Oil it!

Draw some holes in the cheese to make it look more interesting.

Finish the details of the head — whiskers, buck teeth, and a little fringe above the eyes.

Now you can ink in your outlines, adding shadows under the mouse and his feast. Yummy!

What do you get when you cross a mouse with an elephant?

Huge holes in the skirting-boards.

Butch the Dog

Dogs come in a greater variety of shapes and sizes than any other kind of animal. With cartoon dogs, the range is even wider! You can draw a dog as cute as the heroine of *Lady and the Tramp*, or as butch as the feller below.

Start with a long oval, add a peak on top, and take down two curving shoulders rather like a cape.

Add these two big tear-shapes for ears. They don't have to be attached to the head!

Add two small circles for beady eyes.

Make the arms thin and bendy like pipe-cleaners for a comic contrast with the big body.

Now give him a big bone to gloat over, and a thick collar.

Between the nose and the collar, draw in a wide smile, with the tongue hanging out at the thought of that juicy bone.

Finish drawing the details of the head, with a tuft of fur on top.

Ink or paint the ears and nose black, leaving a white highlight on each to make them look rounded and shiny.

Why is it hard to find a dog going cheap?

Because they usually go woof!

Give your dog a firm grip on his bone by curving his 'fingers' around the ends.

Mole in a Hole

Living underground, the mole doesn't need good eyesight: he is nearly blind. What he does need is good digging tools, so he has huge hands which he uses like spades. He is drawn here peeping out of his molehill — he wouldn't be happy away from it.

Start with these two shapes — the molehill, and a 'shark's fin' shape for the mole's head.

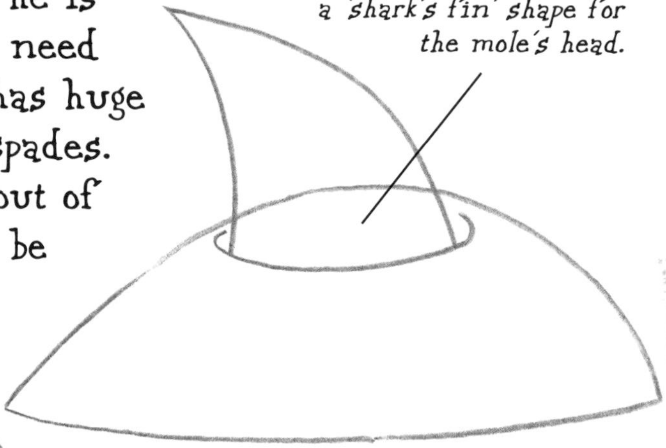

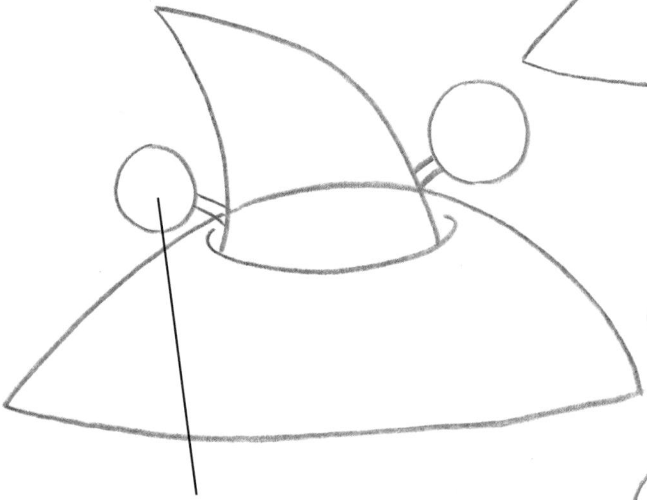

Add two thin little arms, ending in big circles as guidelines for the mole's large hands.

Four small circles form nose, eyes, and an ear.

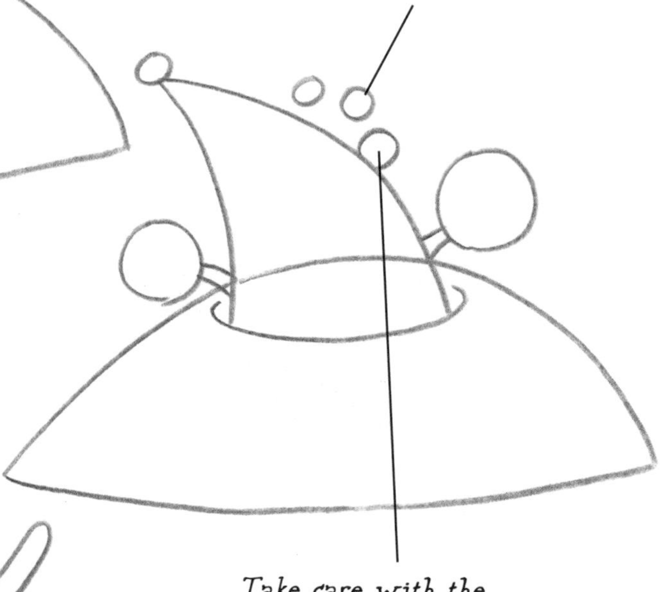

Take care with the spacing of these circles.

The hands become bigger when you add fat, sausage-like fingers and thumbs. Join the two eye circles, and add a curved arm to make them into eyeglasses sitting just above the face.

Give your mole a small, smiley mouth — about halfway down the 'shark's fin' shape.

Start inking in your outlines. Add a few whiskers around the nose. Use a bold curving line to mark out the lighter-colored chest fur — the mole's 'velvet waistcoat.'

Finish off your drawing by turning the mound into a real molehill, with lumps and bumps and rough edges. A few tiny clods of earth flying from the mole's outstretched hands show that work is in progress!

Moles seem to delight in throwing up their hills in the middle of the smoothest lawns, or the most carefully tended flower beds. You may like to draw some collapsing flowers round the mound.

Mrs Kangaroo

Kangaroos, of course, are famous for having invented the pocket and turned it into a portable nursery. Mind you, it's tough on a kangaroo mother. As she says, 'I hate it when it's raining and the kids have to play inside!'

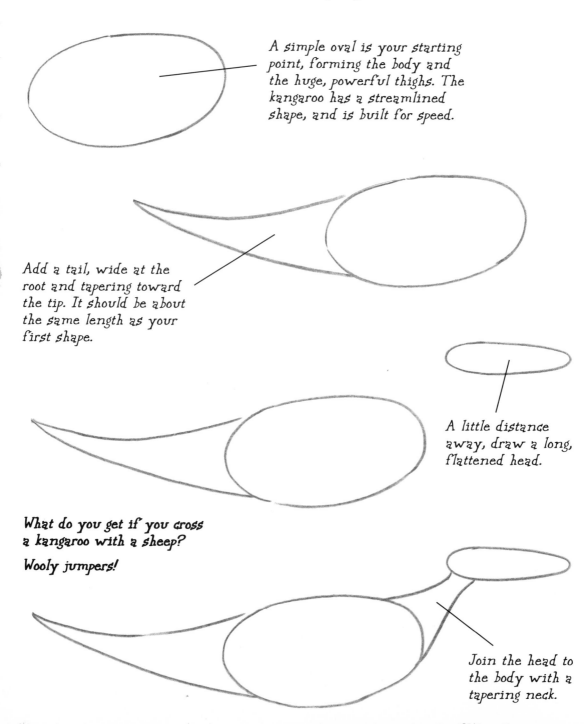

A simple oval is your starting point, forming the body and the huge, powerful thighs. The kangaroo has a streamlined shape, and is built for speed.

Add a tail, wide at the root and tapering toward the tip. It should be about the same length as your first shape.

A little distance away, draw a long, flattened head.

What do you get if you cross a kangaroo with a sheep?

Wooly jumpers!

Join the head to the body with a tapering neck.

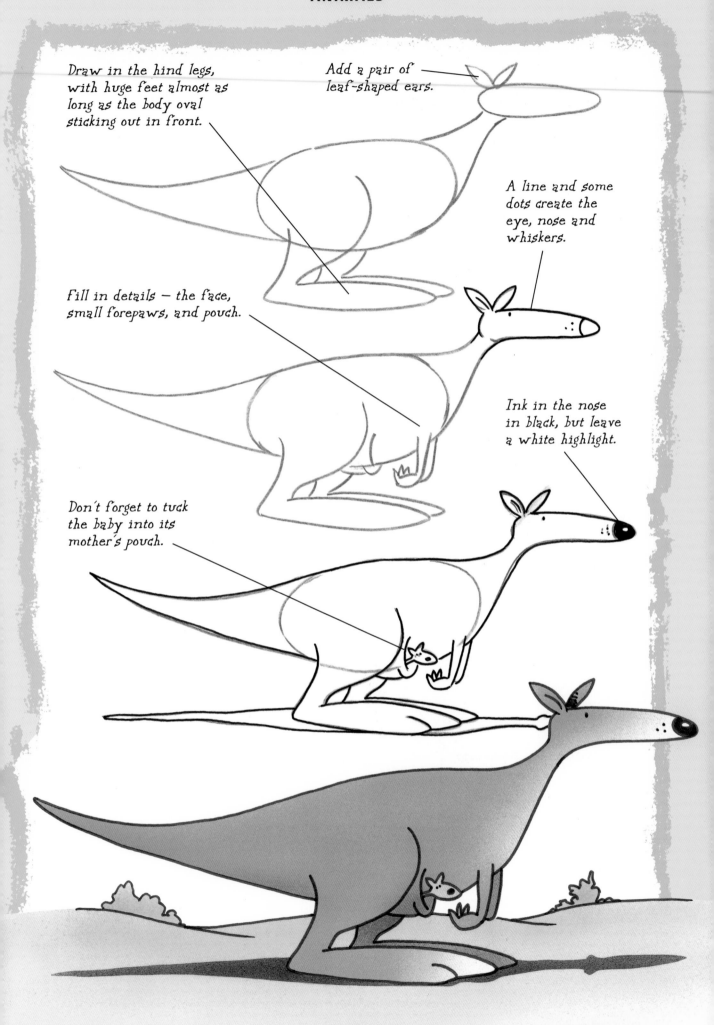

Draw in the hind legs, with huge feet almost as long as the body oval sticking out in front.

Add a pair of leaf-shaped ears.

A line and some dots create the eye, nose and whiskers.

Fill in details — the face, small forepaws, and pouch.

Ink in the nose in black, but leave a white highlight.

Don't forget to tuck the baby into its mother's pouch.

Pretty Polly!

Parrots are noted for their beautiful colors and their ability to talk. Just as striking is the parrot's beak, which serves as a multi-purpose tool-kit — nutcracker, pliers, grappling hook, etc. Its size and shape make this beak a cartoonist's dream.

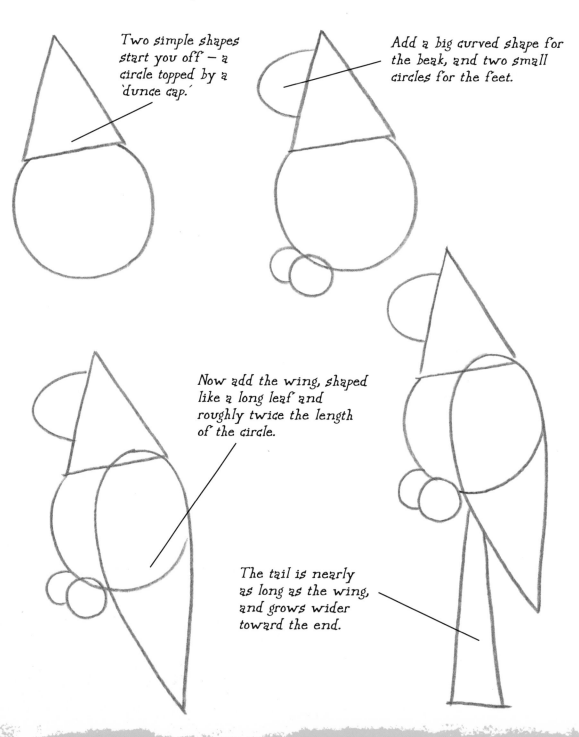

Two simple shapes start you off — a circle topped by a 'dunce cap.'

Add a big curved shape for the beak, and two small circles for the feet.

Now add the wing, shaped like a long leaf and roughly twice the length of the circle.

The tail is nearly as long as the wing, and grows wider toward the end.

Give your parrot a perch to sit on, and add a large eye and a crest on top of the head.

Shape the head, curving the neck and forming a sharp, hook-shaped beak.

Fill in details — feathers, toes, etc. — and don't forget the food bowl.

You can have fun with the colors. There are more than 300 varieties of parrots, so that should give you plenty to choose from!

What does a mathematician call a dead parrot?

A polygon!

Merry Reindeer

It's impossible to think of reindeer without thinking of Christmas and red-nosed Rudolph. But they do more than pull Santa's sleigh. In the frozen north where they live, they also pull buses, mail vehicles, and even army gear.

Start with a big triangle crossed by a large oval which will become your reindeer's nose.

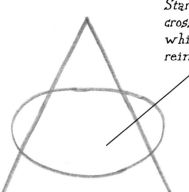

Now you have the basis of the head and that great big nose.

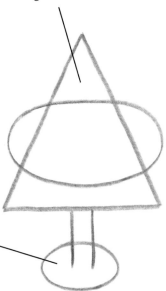

Add a skinny neck (yes, it does look a bit like a Christmas tree now!) and a circle at the base which will form a collar.

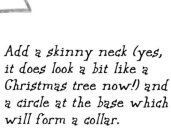

These two circles will make the eyes.

Two large, leaf-shaped ears are drawn from the edges of the eyes. Finish sketching in a collar at the base of the neck.

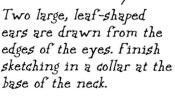

Draw in big antlers, with a tuft of hair between.

Now work in details, using your early lines as a guide. Extend the curves of the cheeks and jaw to bulge out beyond the nose.

Two lines create heavy eyelids, and give our reindeer a pleasantly dopey expression.

Add a few freckles for whiskers, and finish off the collar with a bell.

Don't forget to color your reindeer's nose in bright red, to match Santa's costume.

Gymnast

When you watch gymnasts in action, they move with grace and confidence. The humor in this cartoon comes from the absence of those very qualities. This gymnast looks like he's having real trouble clearing the vaulting horse.

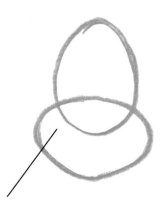

Be careful how you space these ovals for the feet.

Start with an egg shape for the head, and this second shape for the shoulders and chest.

Adding hair and ears turns the 'egg' into a recognizable head.

Slightly curved arms reach down to grip the top of the vaulting horse.

Finish drawing the vaulting horse, and link the feet to the body with chubby legs.

Draw in legs on the shorts and shoes.

A simple line for the mouth can still be very expressive.

Keep clothes simple. Short curved lines help to suggest the shape of the body inside.

Hands and feet don't need to be drawn in any great detail.

Draw your outlines slightly thicker under chin, legs of shorts, chest, etc. to suggest shadows.

Hockey Player

Movements are exaggerated in the cartoon world. So an awkward lunge at the ball in real life becomes very awkward indeed when we draw it. Making the hockey player squat and chunky, rather than fit and lean, emphasizes the comic effect.

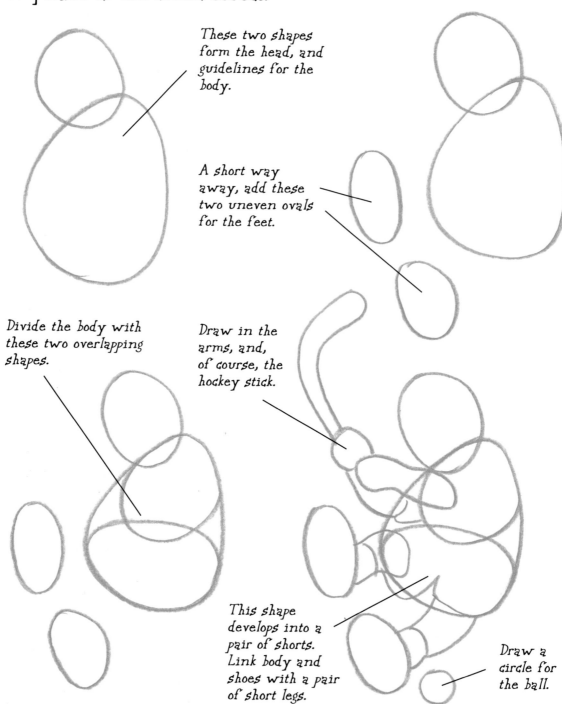

These two shapes form the head, and guidelines for the body.

A short way away, add these two uneven ovals for the feet.

Divide the body with these two overlapping shapes.

Draw in the arms, and, of course, the hockey stick.

This shape develops into a pair of shorts. Link body and shoes with a pair of short legs.

Draw a circle for the ball.

Draw in hair and face. A lopsided mouth gives a look of intense concentration.

Start to ink in your outlines.

Shirt and shorts are made up of a series of simple curves.

The hands are simplified — cartoon characters often have only three fingers like this.

Little bows on the clumpy shoes add a comic touch.

Ice Skater

Drawing someone who is ill-suited to their chosen sport, like a small, weedy weightlifter, is another way of making a comic picture. Here we have a skater with all the grace of a hippopotamus!

Start with an egg shape for the head.

This circle forms the chubby body.

Position this large oval overlapping the body circle just below the center. Believe it or not, this is nearly all the guideline you need for the legs!

Position the feet. One just overlaps the lower shape, and the other is its own length below it.

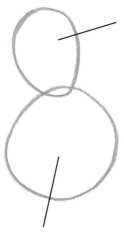

When you draw in hair, plump arms, and huge, wobbly legs, the whole figure starts to appear.

Draw the face, leaving plenty of room for a nice set of double chins.

The arms are raised in what would be a graceful arch if they were more shapely.

Draw the skirt hem as a wavy line that spreads out beyond her fat thighs.

Add a few broken rings to show the skate marks — and let's hope she isn't skating on thin ice!

Make the skates big and rather shapeless — not for dainty little feet!

Where does a mouse go to skate?

The mice rink!

Tennis Player

Some people play sports for fun. Others play to win! You can see which kind this tennis player is! But only half the story is told by his expression of manic determination. His tense, twisted posture is just as important.

The egg-shaped head is tilted one way, looking toward the ball. . .

. . . while the longer oval for the body tilts more strongly in the other direction.

Make the two shapes for the outstretched thighs slightly different in size and form. This one is shorter, because this leg faces toward us a little more.

Draw an oval for the tennis racket, slanting it at an angle. Make it nearly as big as the player's head.

This shape is the start of an outstretched arm.

The large feet, tucked under the body, are roughly bean-shaped. Be careful with your spacing, leaving room to fit in the calves of his legs.

Draw in his face, taking the chin out beyond your oval guideline so that it juts out fiercely. The nose is smelling victory!

The arm holding the racket is twisted right across the body. Draw it in sections — elbow, wristband, and clenched fist.

The other arm is outstretched for balance.

Adding patterns and fastenings turns the bean-shaped feet into a pair of great big sneakers.

Patient: After the operation, will I be able to play tennis?

Surgeon: Of course you will!

Patient: That's great, because I never could before!

Soccer Player

We call it soccer or football — but one of its high points might well be called headball! Action pictures are always fun to draw. Here we have a soccer star caught at the moment when he leaps into the air to head the ball.

Start with these two egg shapes, for the head and chest. Don't forget to leave a space between them for a neck.

This shape, rather like the cap of a toadstool, is placed off-center at the base of the chest, and will form the tops of the legs.

Add a circle for the ball, just above the player's head.

This arm stretches out. For the other arm, only the hand and wrist extend beyond your oval shape.

Three more shapes complete the outline of the bent legs. Only one foot is visible at this angle.

Because his head is tipped back toward the ball, set the features high on the face, with the smiling mouth roughly at the center.

An extra curve makes his soccer shirt swing loosely out from his body, increasing the impression of movement.

Some symmetrical lines make up the sections of the soccer.

Soccer boots don't need a lot of definition. Just add a simple pattern and laces — and the essential studs.

Choose the shirt color of your favorite team, or make up one of your own.

Hurdler

Some people think that fences should be seen and not hurdled! Others float gracefully over them. Here, however, we have a hurdler who is making a bit of a mess of it. Still, he gets full marks for effort.

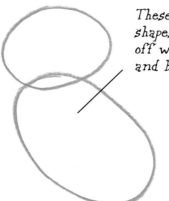

These two rounded shapes start you off with head and body.

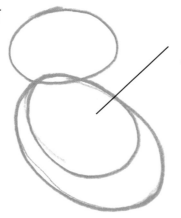

This inner oval marks out the division between vest and shorts.

Add this blob for one leg, which is bent behind the runner and so appears short. Draw a longer, sausage-like shape for the leading leg.

This bulge gives you part of the right arm, mostly hidden behind the runner. Draw the other arm swinging forward, and add big, shapeless feet to the legs.

Now the whole figure is sketched in, you can add the hurdles — which he is only just clearing. The back hurdle is drawn on a slant, as it is toppling over. Too close for comfort!

The face fits within your original oval: you only need add a small bulge for the nose. Add a curve to suggest the puffed-out cheeks.

Making the hair stream jaggedly behind him is an effective way of giving the impression of speed.

His hand is clenched into a fist with the effort of hurdling.

A couple of creases add shape to his running vest.

Who was the fastest runner in history?

Adam, of course. He was the first in the human race.

Cricketer

Cricket can be a dangerous game, as this batsman has just discovered. He has hit the ball fair and square, but the ball doesn't seem to observe the rules of the game! Perhaps the bowler used a cannonball by mistake!

Two slanting ovals form the batsman's head and body.

Add two elongated ovals to outline his legs. The back leg is slightly shorter, because of the angle at which we see it.

Shape this arm carefully, setting the elbow halfway down the body. Padded gloves make the hands big and rather shapeless.

Finish off his legs which are protected by pads, and add large feet.

Behind the two lumpy gloves, these two shapes form his other arm and sleeve.

Draw the bat, with a hole in the middle.

Draw round, staring eyes and a mouth twisted in dismay.

Shape the large pads that are made of individual sections.

The wind of the ball's flight has flicked up his collar.

Even the wicket is falling apart with surprise!

Canoeist

Water provides opportunities for all sorts of sports, from water-skiing to fishing. Paddling your own canoe is one way to enjoy yourself on the water. Being pursued by sharks isn't! Put the two together and you have an unusual experience! Jaws with oars!

Start with the head and body and then, a little way off, outline the blades of the paddle.

Next, draw in the hollow canopy of the canoe.

Start the right arm at the center of the body, with the left one just above it.

Make the bunches of hair slightly uneven.

Curve the lower part of the body where it fits into the canoe seat.

Diver

Water gives us a lot of images in everyday speech. We say that people 'dive into' things when they are keen, or 'dip a toe in the water' when they are slow and cautious. Faced with real water, this diver is managing to do both!

Under a longish head, this shape (like a triangle with rounded corners) forms the bent body.

Draw a large oval across the body — the rubber ring which this nervous swimmer won't dive without!

Draw a curve, roughly a third of the way down the body, to form the upper part of an arm.

Complete the arms, with hands pressed together ready to dive. Or is he praying!

Add the legs and feet. One big toe reaches timidly toward the water, while the other toes shrink away.

Draw in the worried face, an old fashioned bathing cap, and goggles.

A skinny neck links the head to sloping shoulders.

Draw in the diving board, curling the toes of one foot gingerly round its edge.

When you ink in your final lines, make sure that the diver's leg and elbow overlap the rubber ring.

Our neighbor drained all the water from his swimming pool.

'Why did you do that?' we asked.

He said, 'I want to practice diving, but the water's too cold!'

Weightlifter

Weightlifting is an increasingly popular form of exercise today. Not all weightlifters are muscle-bound hunks who strain at huge weights. Here we have one who is really enjoying herself — watch out, Wondergirl!

Start with the head and body, slightly overlapping one another.

Leave a space between the body and the arms, where you can draw in sleeves later.

Draw the thighs as two longish ovals at the base of the figure.

Draw this weight round, and the one at the other end oval.

Shape the upper body, curving it inward to a trim waist.

Wiggly lines for the legs prepare the way for folds in the tracksuit botoms.

Use jagged lines to form a mane of shaggy hair behind a sweatband.

Add creases to the sleeves and waist of the T-shirt.

The curved bar of the weights is reflected in the curve of the weightlifter's thighs. This creates a balance between the top and bottom of the drawing.

Curve the arms slightly at the elbows. The big smile tells it all!

Footballer

Football is a rough, tough contact sport. The players look hugely powerful in their protective clothing. But sometimes people who are tough on the outside can be quite timid really, when faced with a spider — or a mouse!

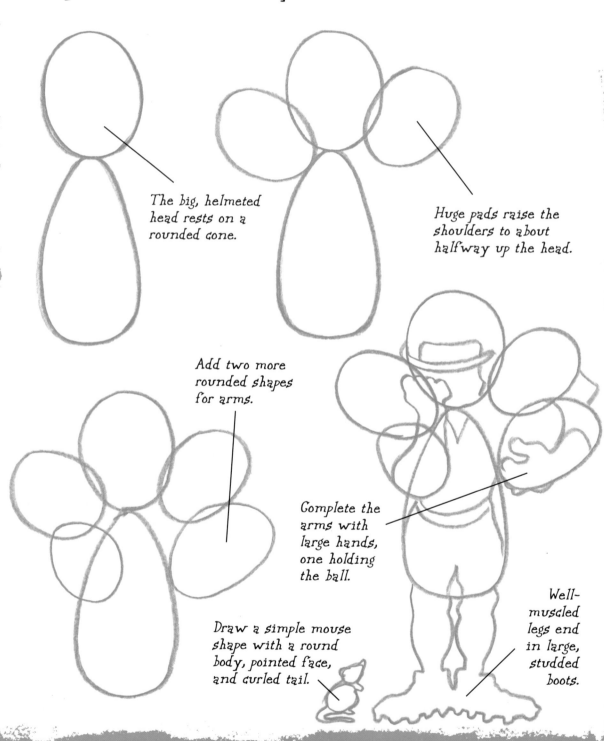

The big, helmeted head rests on a rounded cone.

Huge pads raise the shoulders to about halfway up the head.

Add two more rounded shapes for arms.

Complete the arms with large hands, one holding the ball.

Well-muscled legs end in large, studded boots.

Draw a simple mouse shape with a round body, pointed face, and curled tail.

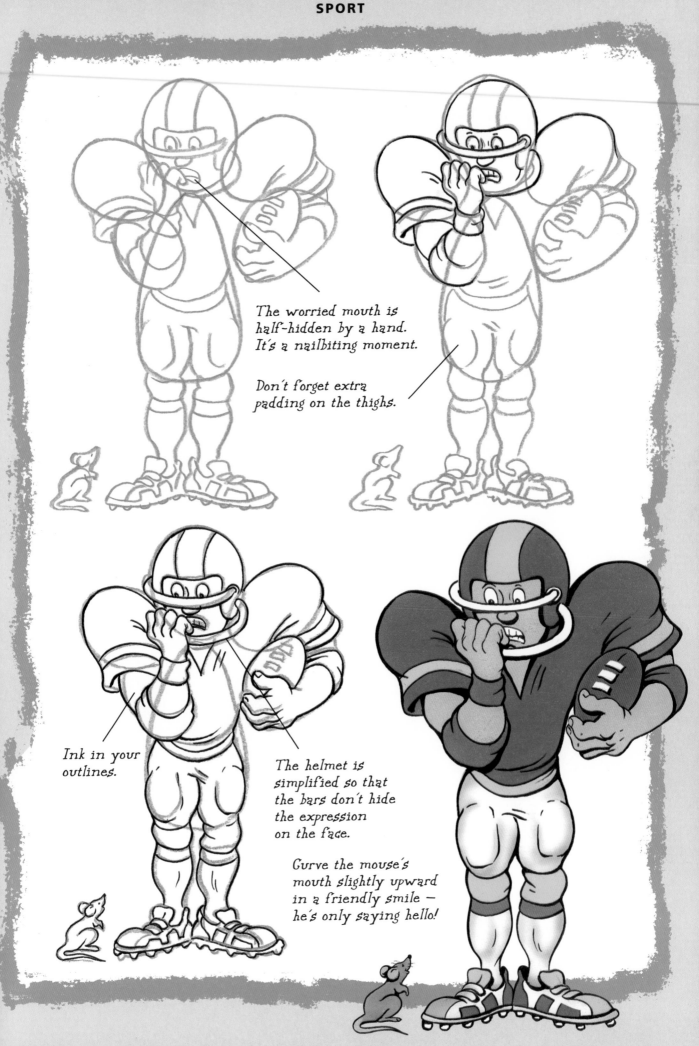

The worried mouth is half-hidden by a hand. It's a nailbiting moment.

Don't forget extra padding on the thighs.

Ink in your outlines.

The helmet is simplified so that the bars don't hide the expression on the face.

Curve the mouse's mouth slightly upward in a friendly smile — he's only saying hello!

Skier

When things go wrong on the sports field, the cartoonist leaps in with glee. But someone having a good time enjoying their favorite sport can also make a great cartoon. All you have to do is exaggerate a little!

A rough circle forms the head.

Extend this shape (shoulder and arm) down almost to the lower edge of the body.

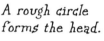

Overlapping the edge of the head, the body leans at an angle to crouch over the skis.

Add a raised arm. Draw a large shape for the hand, because of the thick gloves.

One ski stick waves joyfully in the air, while the other is tucked under the other arm.

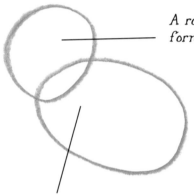

These two shapes for the thighs slant slightly upward toward the back of the body.

The large feet extend beyond each knee, and are set into bindings on narrow skis.

Draw the face, with a wide happy grin. In real life, the shades would cover his eyes — but we want to be able to see his gleeful expression.

Curved creases in his ski pants suggest the shape of the legs beneath. Add some more creases in his jacket as well.

Curly hair is easy to draw, with lots of small bubbly curves.

Skiing is easy. You can learn how to do it in just a few sittings!

Basketball Player

All sorts of things can go wrong on the basketball court. Here, the idea is to get the ball in the basket. However, it seems this player has got it all wrong. Either that, or he must be a bit of a basket case!

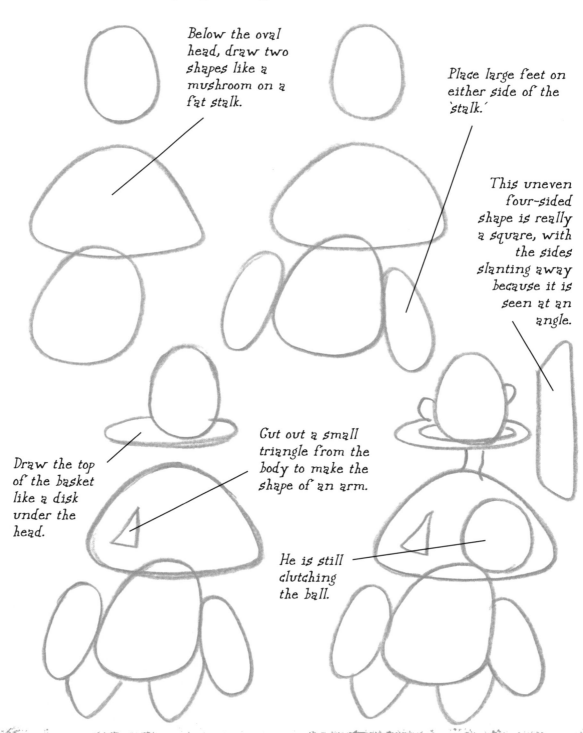

Below the oval head, draw two shapes like a mushroom on a fat stalk.

Place large feet on either side of the 'stalk.'

This uneven four-sided shape is really a square, with the sides slanting away because it is seen at an angle.

Draw the top of the basket like a disk under the head.

Cut out a small triangle from the body to make the shape of an arm.

He is still clutching the ball.

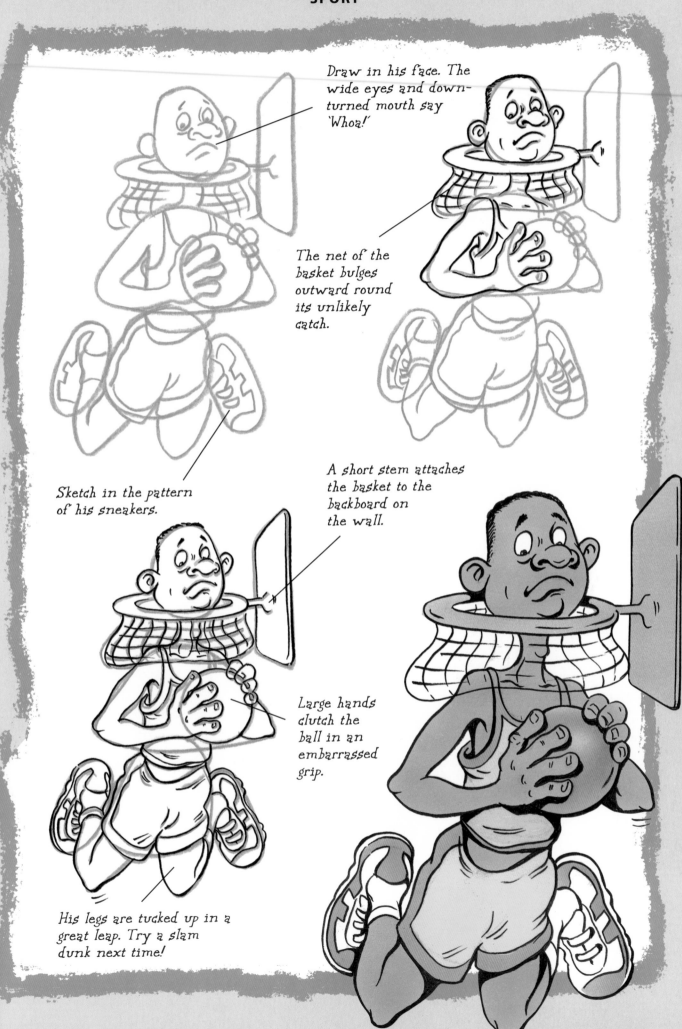

Draw in his face. The wide eyes and down-turned mouth say 'Whoa!'

The net of the basket bulges outward round its unlikely catch.

Sketch in the pattern of his sneakers.

A short stem attaches the basket to the backboard on the wall.

Large hands clutch the ball in an embarrassed grip.

His legs are tucked up in a great leap. Try a slam dunk next time!

Rugby Player

You don't have to draw a whole rugby team to capture the speed and excitement of the game. One player in action is enough to represent all of them. Of course, it helps to exaggerate his brute strength.

This circle isn't his head, but his powerful shoulder, thrusting for the line.

These two odd shapes form his body, twisted as he changes direction.

This is the head, with bulging cheeks puffed out to the sides.

Add the bent arm, cradling the ball in a giant grasp.

His large feet are positioned well to the side. Leave a good space for the legs.

Link the feet to the body with strong, muscular legs.

The clenched jaw stretches his face into a grimace of exertion.

The wide sleeve balloons out round his arm.

Draw in his socks and rugby boots.

His hair stands up in a crown of spikes.

The H-shaped goalposts are just visible behind his shoulder.

The twist of his body, pushing ahead of his legs, adds to the impression of speed.

Surfer

Sun, sea, and sand will do for most of us. But for athletic types like this guy, it has to be sun, sea, and surf! It takes a good sense of balance, but you're never bored with a board while there are waves to ride.

The head perches on a body that is leaning back to maintain his balance.

The two oval shapes for his thighs come to a point at the knees. They are both bigger than the head, because they are nearer to us in this view.

A little way below the thigh, add the outline of a foot, placed sideways.

This blunt-cornered triangle will help you to position his bent arm, raised toward his head.

When you draw this outstretched arm, place it so that the shoulder pushes upward from the body, to emphasize the muscles.

Only one end of the surfboard emerges from the rolling waves. finish shaping the legs, and add a wave breaking over the back of the board.

Windswept hair streams behind him. Now you can add detail to the bent arm, curling the fingers round into a clenched fist.

Draw in the face, making the huge, happy grin the main feature. Don't forget the dimple in his chin. What a dude!

Draw splashing waves all around the surfboard, and add a few flying, tear-shaped drops of water.

Give him a muscular chest to match the curving muscles of his arms and legs. (But he can still have knobbly knees.)

Why do surfers never have hidden depths?

Because they're all surf aces!

Complete his feet with broad toes, bracing themselves on the curved board.

Golfer

Golf takes a lot of concentration. Watch a golfer studying his ball, choosing his line, and finally making a swing, and you will find many opportunities for cartoons. The amount of effort going into this shot is staggering, in all senses!

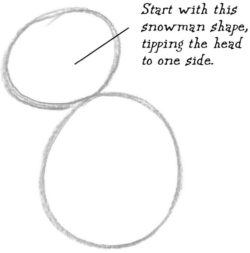

Start with this snowman shape, tipping the head to one side.

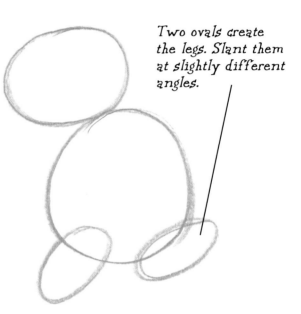

Two ovals create the legs. Slant them at slightly different angles.

A curve between head and body begins to form a raised arm.

Complete this leg with a rounded blob for the shin, and a raised foot above it.

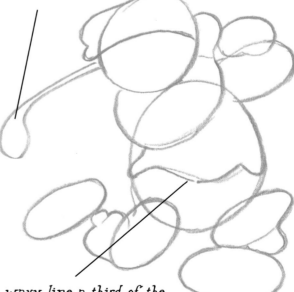

The power of his swing takes his golf club right behind his head.

A wavy line a third of the way up his body marks the bottom of his waistcoat.

Draw in his face. Three short curving lines form one eye screwed shut in concentration, while the other eye is wide and round.

His fingers are curled tightly round the handle of the golf club.

The loose trousers fall into curves and folds before tucking into the socks. The ankles are comically thin above large golf shoes.

When the doctor told my father to go out and play thirty-six holes a day, I don't think he understood.

Pop went out and bought a harmonica!

Pegasus

In Greek myth, the winged horse Pegasus roams the skies freely. Only the gods and (with their permission) heroes dare ride him. But the cartoon world can be a gentler place, where he becomes a happy colt scampering among the clouds.

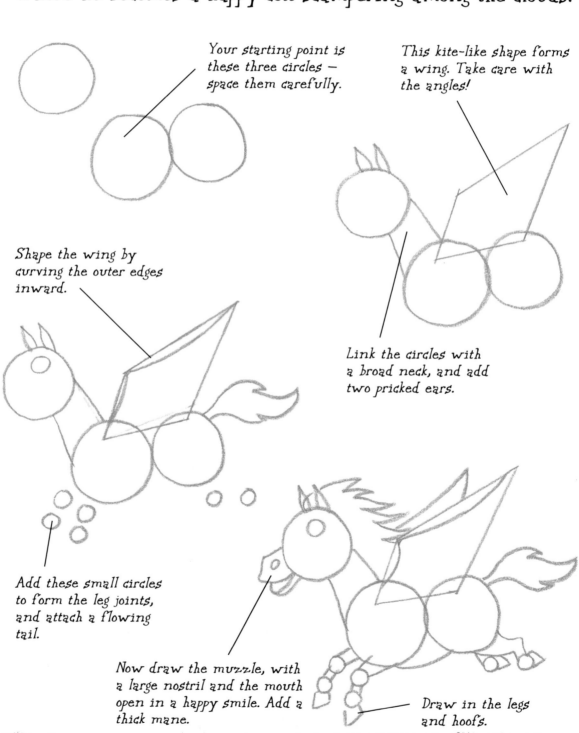

Your starting point is these three circles — space them carefully.

This kite-like shape forms a wing. Take care with the angles!

Shape the wing by curving the outer edges inward.

Link the circles with a broad neck, and add two pricked ears.

Add these small circles to form the leg joints, and attach a flowing tail.

Now draw the muzzle, with a large nostril and the mouth open in a happy smile. Add a thick mane.

Draw in the legs and hoofs.

Curve the join between muzzle and head, and draw in details of eyes, ears, and wings. Short lines beside the wings and tails give the impression of movement.

Finish drawing the head and shaggy mane.

Fluffy clouds adorn the skies which are Pegasus's playground.

Shape the base of the wing where it sprouts from the shoulder, and ink in your outlines.

Cartoon animals often have large heads to make a stronger impact. The downward glance in the eye helps give an impression that Pegasus is flying high.

Cupid

The Roman god of love, Cupid, is a mischievous child. He shoots his golden arrows at people to make them fall in love, often choosing the most unlikely couples, just for fun. Today we still use images of Cupid on Valentine's cards.

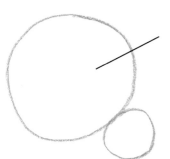

Start with a large circle for the head, and a smaller one which will make the front part of the body.

Position these two small circles, for the hands, carefully, the left one a little lower than the right.

Add another circle, slightly overlapping the first body section and just a little smaller.

Two small ovals, overlapping the second body section, make Cupid's thighs. Little arms link the hands to the body, and two more small circles, low on the face, form chubby cheeks.

Cupid's natural habitat is in the heavens, so add a couple of clouds.

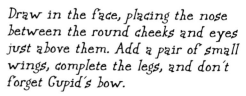

Draw in the face, placing the nose between the round cheeks and eyes just above them. Add a pair of small wings, complete the legs, and don't forget Cupid's bow.

Start filling in details: Cupid's curly hair, his hands, and wing feathers running in two rows.

Finish drawing the face, giving Cupid an expression of cheeky mischief.

Draw the arrow just leaving the bow. Cupid's left hand has only just fired it, so indicate the hand's movement with a couple of little curved 'spin marks' in front of it.

Use curved 'spin marks' again to indicate movement, this time of Cupid's wings.

The two cheek circles form guidelines for the placement and spacing of his other features.

Cupid's head is drawn much bigger than his body. Sometimes he is drawn without any body at all — just a head, wings and, of course, hands to hold his golden bow.

Bad Fairy

Long ago, bad fairies were really scary. People blamed them for any illness or bad luck, and dreaded offending them. Today the Bad Fairy belongs only in fairy stories and pantomimes, where her wicked ways are always easily defeated.

The head is a fat oval — not a circle! Draw a curved line across it, about a third of the way down.

Add a small, solid body and two bent 'stick' arms.

A big 'shark's fin' shape forms the hat.

Draw a big topless triangle to make guidelines for the wings, and add 'stick' legs.

Now start adding details. Shape the arms, legs, and hat, draw in the wings, and add slanted eyes and a snub nose.

The slant of the evil grin matches that of the eyes.

The huge hat adds to the comic, cartoon effect. Its pointy shape also suggests the hat of another fairy-tale baddie, the Wicked Witch.

Draw the hair with jagged, spiky lines as you ink in your cartoon.

Keep the feet small, with simple boots.

fairy wings are transparent, like those of an insect.

Good Fairy

With a wave of her magic wand, the Good Fairy makes everything come right. Let's draw her and her wand in action. Cartoon actions are always exaggerated, so she bends and braces herself as if the wand were a big, heavy club.

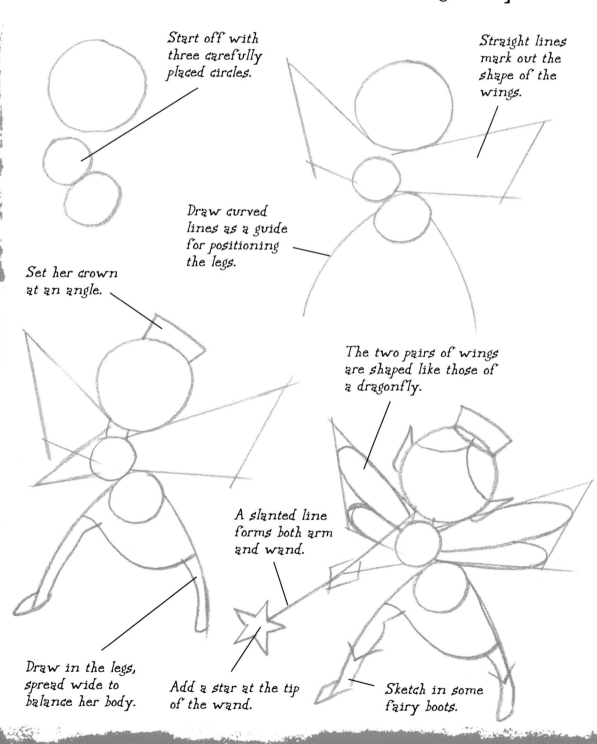

Start off with three carefully placed circles.

Straight lines mark out the shape of the wings.

Draw curved lines as a guide for positioning the legs.

Set her crown at an angle.

The two pairs of wings are shaped like those of a dragonfly.

A slanted line forms both arm and wand.

Draw in the legs, spread wide to balance her body.

Add a star at the tip of the wand.

Sketch in some fairy boots.

Her head is tilted, so draw eyes and mouth on a slant.

Curve her dress smoothly around her legs.

Wide, level eyes, a small nose, and a smiling mouth make up a very different face from the Bad Fairy's.

A trail of little sparkling stars shows the wand's movement.

Both hands meet at the end of the wand.

Bad Fairies have to wear black or dark shades, but white or light colors form the Good Fairy's 'uniform.'

Genie of the Lamp

When Aladdin rubbed his magic lamp, out came the Genie to grant his wishes. And here he comes again, in a puff of smoke.

The circles and curved line establish the arms and hands.

Draw the head first, with a large 'slice' marked out to separate face from turban.

The puff of smoke is nearly as big as his head.

The lamp goes here.

Now link up your three sections and your Genie starts to appear.

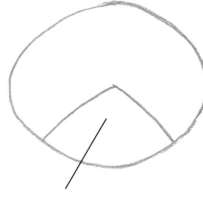

Draw the lamp like a squashed teapot with a long spout.

Give him a happy grin showing big front teeth.

Slanting lines show the folds of his flowing cloak.

Curving the fingers helps to suggest movement.

Use small curves to fluff out the cloud of smoke.

As if by magic your Genie has appeared. 'What is your command, O master?'

Supergirl

Many fantasy figures, like dragons and fairies, date back for centuries. But fantasy isn't stuck in the past. Comic-strip heroes and heroines with super-powers are part of a thriving modern fantasy tradition.

Take care — the head is not a circle but a fat oval.

A long rectangle forms the outstretched body. Short lines cut into it to start creating the body shape.

Add an outflung arm.

The streaming mass of hair is thicker and nearly as long as her body.

Start to shape her body and legs.

Clouds set the scene for her aerobatics.

The large eyes are set just above the center of the face.

Add the collar of her costume, and her other bent arm.

Finish drawing the face. Large features occupy almost all the space.

Complete the feet with a cool pair of boots.

Dimples at the corners of the mouth create a more natural smile than curving the lips.

Her costume is easily sketched in with a few curved lines.

The hands are drawn as closed fists punching through the air.

A few short 'speed lines' behind the figure increase the impression of movement.

Supergirl to the rescue!

Wicked Witch

Cartoon witches are instantly recognizable by their pointy hats. They also have long chins and long noses, warts and claw-like hands. If they aren't flying on a broomstick, they are usually cooking up some horrible spell in a caldron.

These three odd shapes don't look much like a witch yet!

This is less complicated than it looks! A few more lines give you the hat brim, a fall of greasy hair, and two raised hands.

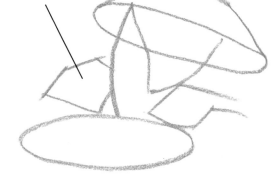

Draw the pointy top of the hat.

Add a big nose, draw in the sleeves and fingers, and suddenly the witch starts to appear.

Turn the lower oval into the rim of a caldron, and add curved sides and a handle. Above it, the Witch's hands hover like bird's claws.

Why did the witch spin round and round?

Because she was having a dizzy spell!

Narrow, curving eyes perch either side of the nose. Sketch in an evil grin, and don't forget the warts!

As you start to ink in your cartoon, make your Wicked Witch look as evil as possible.

Have fun inking in the details, making fingers knobblier and hair stragglier.

A few lumps in the caldron hint at something even worse than school meals!

By drawing the pupils at the outer edges of the eyes, you can make it seem as if the witch is looking — and grinning — directly at you.

What does a witch wear in the kitchen?

Coven gloves!

Tree Goblin

An old rhyme tells us that 'Fairy folks are in old oaks,' and who knows what lives hidden among the trees? This goblin is small enough to wear an acorn cup as a hat, so he would be very hard to spot in his leafy home.

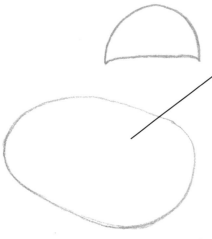

Start with a small half-circle for the acorn-cup hat and, below, a big blobby oval for the goblin's body.

Curved lines will make the shape of the face.

Two small, rough circles mark out the positions of his feet.

Above each foot circle, add a slanting shape for the big toe.

A pair of arms pillow the head. Draw in the rest of the features, and finish the acorn-cup hat with a curved stalk.

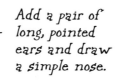

Add a pair of long, pointed ears and draw a simple nose.

Draw the rest of the toes, and sketch in the feet. They are big because they are nearer to us than the head. They also look funny this way!

Fill in the body shape with pointed leaves.

Use simple curved lines for closed eyes. A blissful smile takes up nearly the full width of the face.

Sketch in the lines of branches around the goblin, arranging them so that they form a comfortable nest for him.

A leafy blanket covers the goblin from chin to ankles. Add scratchy lines across the branches of his nest to give the effect of rough bark.

Why didn't the goblin wake up for dinner?

The cook didn't use elf-raising flour!

(Mind you, gobblin' your dinner is bad for your elf!)

Mermaid

Tales of mermaids — half fish, half woman — have been told since ancient times. They are always beautiful, with flowing hair and sweet voices. This is odd, since scientists say the legend was probably inspired by the manatee, or sea cow, a rather unlovely beast!

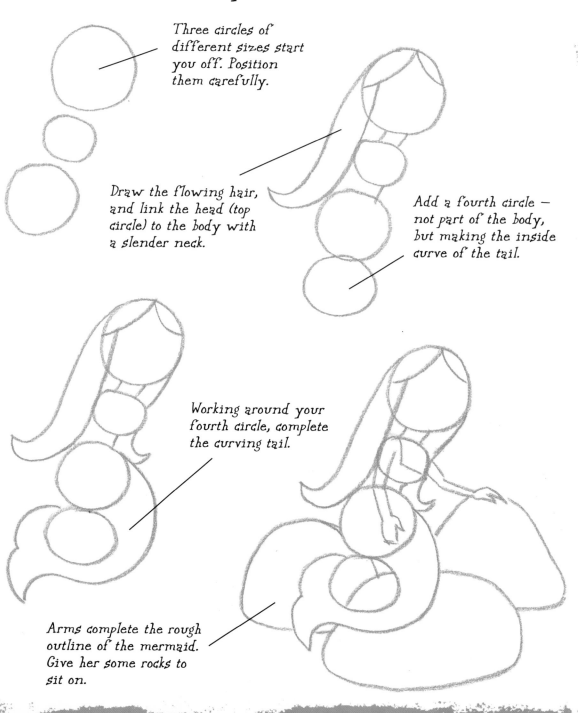

Three circles of different sizes start you off. Position them carefully.

Draw the flowing hair, and link the head (top circle) to the body with a slender neck.

Add a fourth circle — not part of the body, but making the inside curve of the tail.

Working around your fourth circle, complete the curving tail.

Arms complete the rough outline of the mermaid. Give her some rocks to sit on.

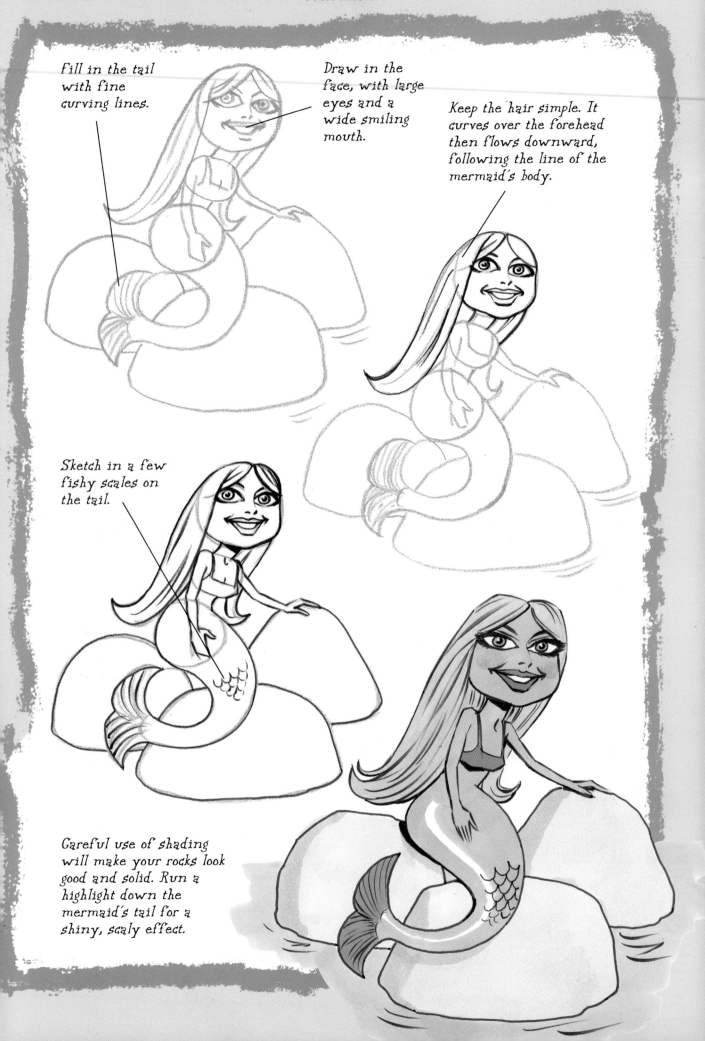

Fill in the tail with fine curving lines.

Draw in the face, with large eyes and a wide smiling mouth.

Keep the hair simple. It curves over the forehead then flows downward, following the line of the mermaid's body.

Sketch in a few fishy scales on the tail.

Careful use of shading will make your rocks look good and solid. Run a highlight down the mermaid's tail for a shiny, scaly effect.

Leprechaun

The Leprechaun — a merry little fellow dressed in green — is the fairy shoemaker of Ireland. If you can catch him, you can demand his secret hoard of gold as the price of his freedom — but he will nearly always manage to escape without paying up.

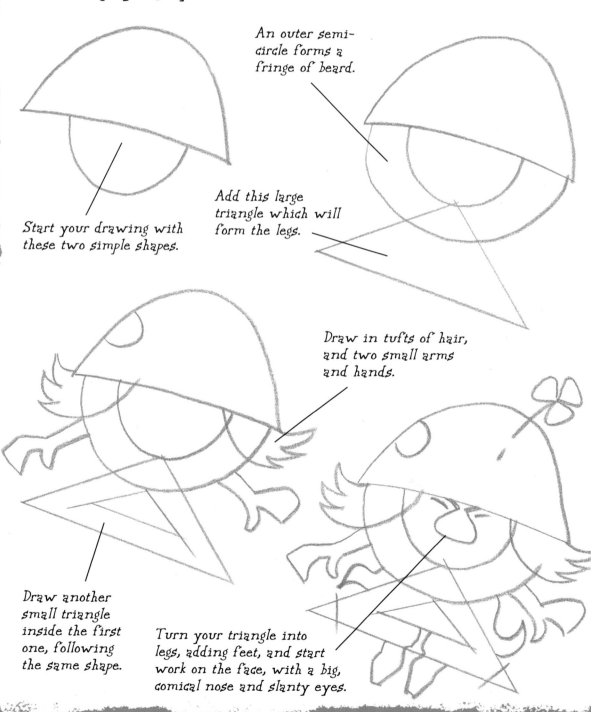

Start your drawing with these two simple shapes.

An outer semi-circle forms a fringe of beard.

Add this large triangle which will form the legs.

Draw in tufts of hair, and two small arms and hands.

Draw another small triangle inside the first one, following the same shape.

Turn your triangle into legs, adding feet, and start work on the face, with a big, comical nose and slanty eyes.

Take a 'bite' out of the hat.

Finish the face with a big, buck-toothed grin, taking the smile lines up to the sides of the nose.

A true Irishman, the Leprechaun has tucked a leaf of Ireland's national plant, the shamrock, into his hat.

Sketch in trousers, creased behind the knee, stockings, and a pair of smart buckled shoes, fit for a champion shoemaker.

Make the hair and beard look suitably 'wild and wooly.'

Notice that you didn't need to draw the Leprechaun's body, only his legs. Hidden by his beard, it is suggested by his flying coat-tails.

Centaur

Centaurs — half man and half horse — belong to ancient legend. They are often said to be great hunters, skilled with bow and arrow. This is why the star sign Sagittarius, 'the Archer,' is usually shown in pictures as a centaur.

These two shapes form the human half of the centaur — head and chest.

The horse's body is formed by a shape similar to the head, but lying on its side.

Divide the face with lines, to help you place the features. Add a mane of hair.

The guidelines give you the positions of eyes, nose, and mouth, as well as mustache and eyebrows.

Draw the centaur's bow.

Add a flowing tail.

Small circles will help you to draw the legs.

A quiver of arrows hangs behind his back, the strap running across his chest.

Thick, boldly curved eyebrows and a full beard give his face a fierce expression.

Marking the joints with circles helps you to shape the legs and hoofs.

Tidy up your outlines as you ink them in.

Have a go at drawing other mythical mixtures — like the griffin, half eagle, half lion!

Magic Carpet

Tales of flying carpets come from the East, where beautiful carpets are woven. This might be a rather drafty form of transport, probably best in hot, dry climates. In rainy weather most of us would prefer an airplane!

Start with these two rounded shapes for the head and body of the 'pilot.'

Two slanted lines start to make his large turban.

Add these two shapes — rather like triangles with rounded corners — for his knees.

Draw in the top of his turban.

Add four slanting lines for the carpet. Be careful with your angles. The back end of the carpet is drawn narrower than the front, because it is farther away from us.

Now you can start adding details. Curl up the ends of the carpet, and give the rider arms and legs. Use curvy lines for his feet, which wear slippers with long, curling toes.

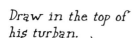

Fill in the face. Round staring eyes make the carpet's rider look just a little bit worried, despite his smile. It's a long way down!

Finish drawing his head, adding a little fringe of beard. A large and splendid ornament fastens his turban.

The turban looks better with a few folds in the cloth, shown by little curving lines.

Clouds help to set the scene up in the sky.

Unlike real life, cartoon people always wear clothes that show exactly who they are. Cooks wear chefs' hats, burglars wear striped jerseys — and flying carpet riders wear full Eastern costume.

Dragon

Dragons are among the oldest inhabitants of the fantasy world. You can have some fun with their fire-breathing habits — this dragon is having problems trying to read a newspaper. He should know about the dangers of smoking!

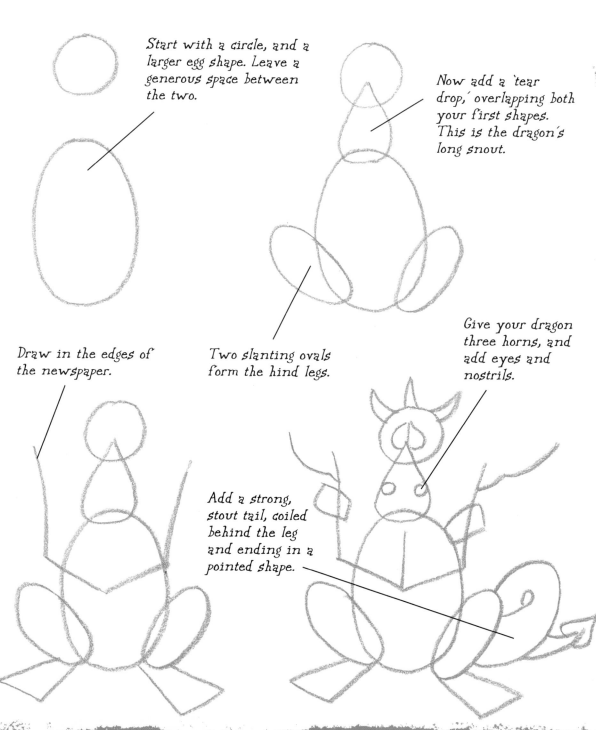

Start with a circle, and a larger egg shape. Leave a generous space between the two.

Now add a 'tear drop,' overlapping both your first shapes. This is the dragon's long snout.

Draw in the edges of the newspaper.

Two slanting ovals form the hind legs.

Give your dragon three horns, and add eyes and nostrils.

Add a strong, stout tail, coiled behind the leg and ending in a pointed shape.

Draw in some flames and smoke, and give your dragon a pair of pointed wings.

Complete the head and shocked face, framed by the charred remains of the newspaper.

Newsprint is shown by simple short lines.

Finish off the feet with long, strong toes and claws.

Today's paper — hot off the press!

Minotaur

In Greek legend, the Minotaur was a fierce brute, half man, half bull. King Minos of Crete kept him in a secret maze, and fed him on human flesh — until the hero Theseus slew him.

Start with these two shapes, and a straight central guideline.

Shape the horns around the top of the head, and add this block.

Add two lines for legs, slightly wider apart at the base.

Using the central guideline, draw in eyes and a broad, heavy muzzle. Add a triangle under the head, as shown.

Add a shaggy fringe and ears to the large, bull-like head.

Small arms hang down below the big head.

This Minotaur doesn't look fierce. The downward curve of the mouth creates the dim, slightly worried expression typical of real cows (and bulls).

A jagged outline frames the huge head in shaggy fur.

The greater the contrast between heavy head and small, thin body, the funnier the cartoon will be.

Goblin

Goblins aren't nice. Small, hideous, and spiteful, they belong to the dark side of the fairy world. In the days before street lights, they lurked on every dark corner.

Start with this shape — an egg with a pointed end — and add a 'skirt.'

Add these four shapes below, for hands and feet.

Start to draw in the goblin's club.

A big lump of a nose and pointed ears help to form a goblin face. Join on the arms, just below the ears.

Shape the shoes, and add little bandy legs.

He carries a simple 'Stone Age' club, ready for action.

The fleshy nose is the key to this face. The upper lip follows its curve, and the eyes tuck in against the top slopes.

Sketch in a small tufty beard.

All the detail is concentrated in the face. The staring eyes look mean. A few sharp teeth hang over the lower lip, ready to give someone a nasty nip.

Keep clothing simple — goblins aren't snazzy dressers!

The angle of the feet and the shortened body make it seem as if we are looking down on the goblin from above. Watch out for your ankles!

Maw

You can make a splendid monster by taking just one feature — from a nose to a foot — and concentrating simply on that. This monster is all mouth, to go with its monster appetite.

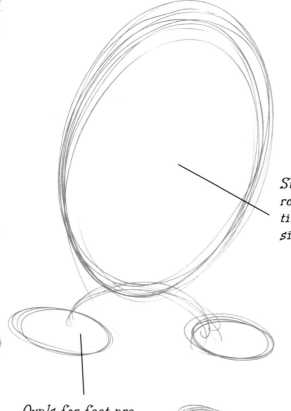

Start with a rough egg shape, tilted to one side.

Ovals for feet are linked to the body by a curved line.

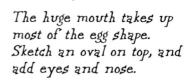

The huge mouth takes up most of the egg shape. Sketch an oval on top, and add eyes and nose.

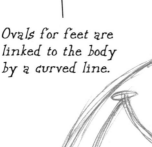

A central circle forms a dangly tonsil. Sketch two rings round it, like a target, to help you build up the inside of the mouth.

Mark out the teeth with large ovals.

Make-believe creatures don't need to have matching eyes. Goggle eyes look great!

These two ovals form the tongue, with a grooved center.

Build up layers within the mouth to give the impression of cavernous depths.

Maw food, please!

The feet are like spanners lying flat on the ground.

Vampire

Horror-story vampires are scary creatures with creepy clothes. Real-life vampires are just bats. They have nothing in common except drinking blood. Our cartoon vampire combines the two: his cloak suggests a bat's wings and tail.

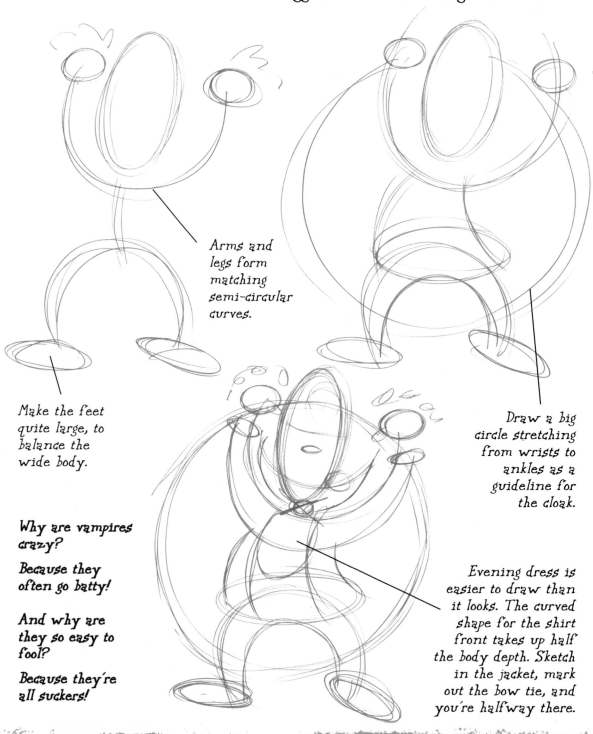

Arms and legs form matching semi-circular curves.

Make the feet quite large, to balance the wide body.

Draw a big circle stretching from wrists to ankles as a guideline for the cloak.

Why are vampires crazy?

Because they often go batty!

And why are they so easy to fool?

Because they're all suckers!

Evening dress is easier to draw than it looks. The curved shape for the shirt front takes up half the body depth. Sketch in the jacket, mark out the bow tie, and you're halfway there.

Draw in the face, filling the lower half with an evil smile. The ear is very low-set for comic effect.

A single eyebrow is the popular style among creatures of the night like vampires and werewolves.

Draw the spread fingers all round the hand for a claw-like effect.

No vampire is complete without his fangs. Very tasty.

What does a polite vampire say after he's bitten you?

'Fangs a lot!'

Scrabber

Some monsters are inspired by real-life beasties. Think of a crab. It's an odd shape to start with — a sort of walking plate with jaws. Multiply the eyes, add some tongues, take away a couple of legs, and what have you got? Well, we've called our monster a Scrabber.

Start with a long oval for the body. Put two small eyes at the front.

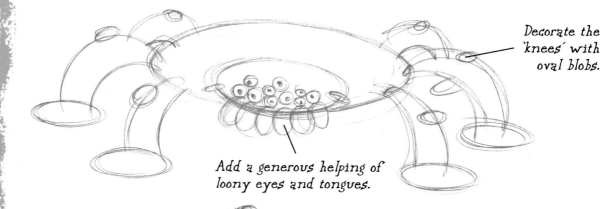

Add half a dozen legs, with big oval feet.

Decorate the 'knees' with oval blobs.

Add a generous helping of loony eyes and tongues.

Sketch in some toes.

Give him a wide, friendly smile — you wouldn't want him to be unfriendly!

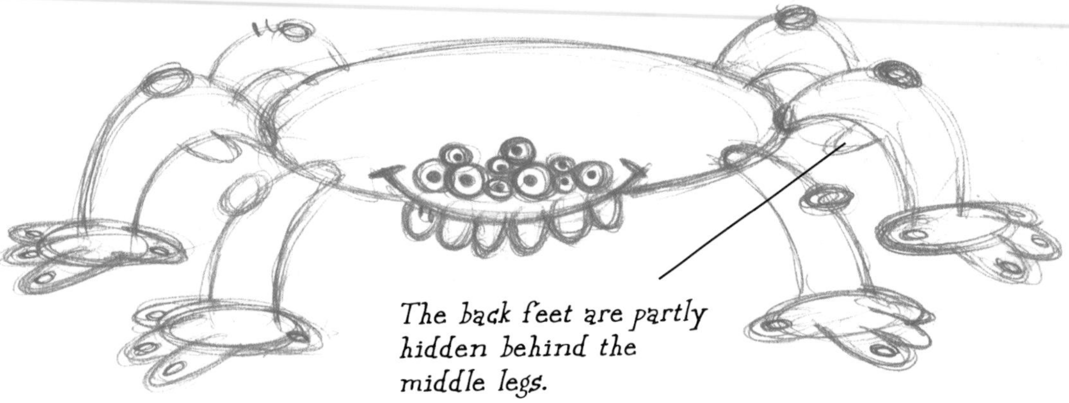

The back feet are partly
hidden behind the
middle legs.

Try out some
toenails — or
maybe
claws.

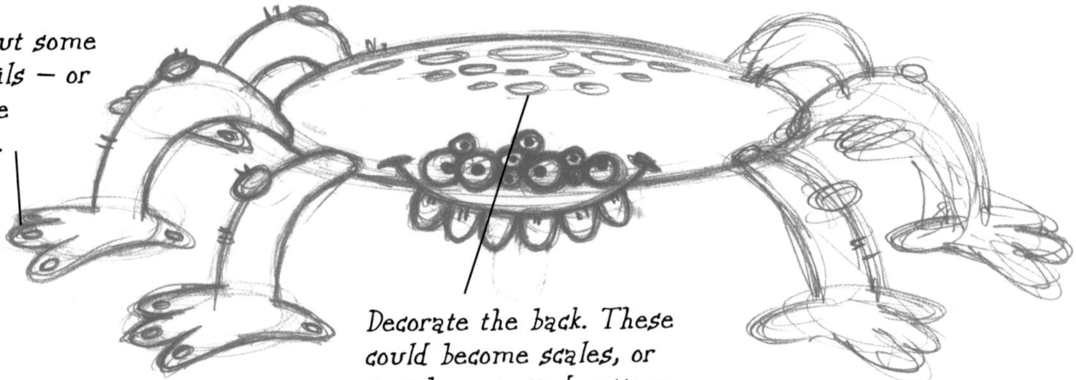

Decorate the back. These
could become scales, or
just be a spotted pattern.

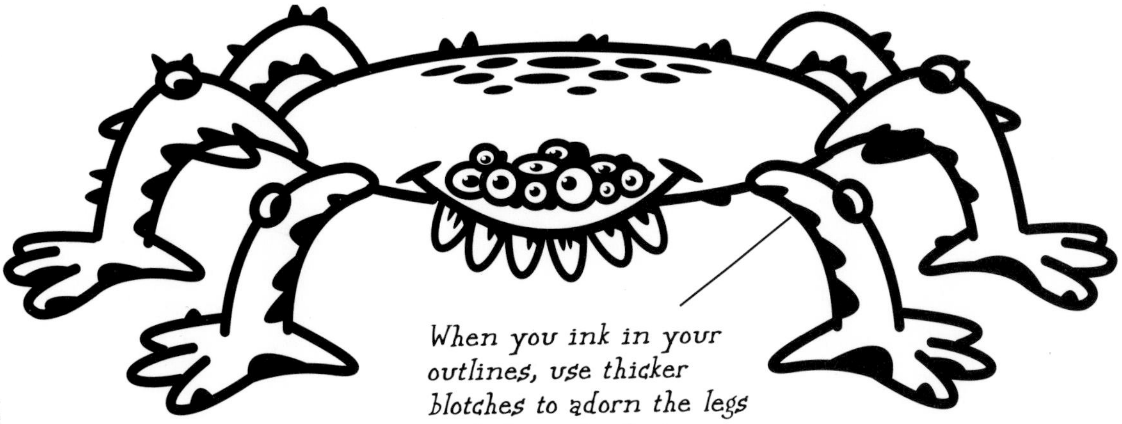

When you ink in your
outlines, use thicker
blotches to adorn the legs
and shape the feet.

A few short spikes on the
back and legs complete
the Scrabber.

Flump

As a general rule, thin spiky monsters look dangerous, and fat rounded ones look cuddly. Try out the thoroughly rounded Flump and see what you think. Cuddly or not, I'm not sure I want to find a Flump lurking under my bed!

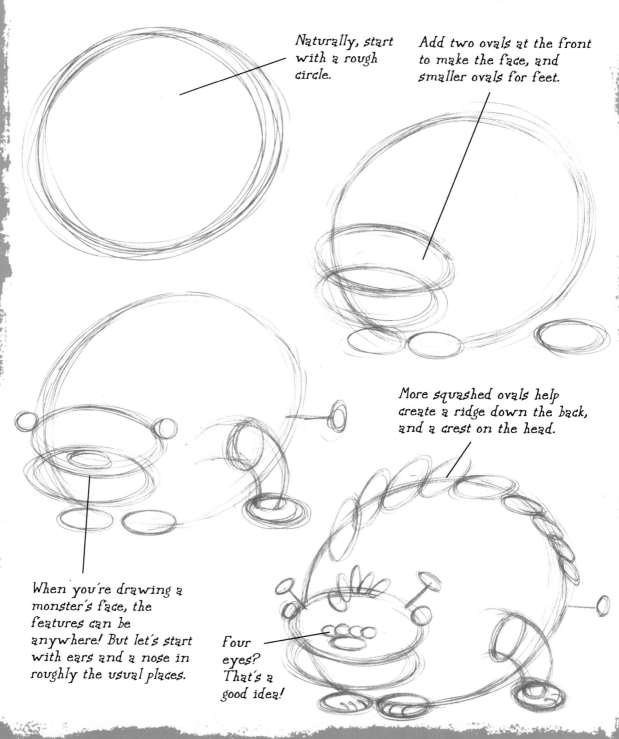

Naturally, start with a rough circle.

Add two ovals at the front to make the face, and smaller ovals for feet.

More *squashed* ovals help create a ridge down the back, and a crest on the head.

When you're drawing a monster's face, the features can be anywhere! But let's start with ears and a nose in roughly the usual places.

Four eyes? That's a good idea!

Finish drawing the head.
A huge, frilly tongue
hanging out of the mouth
makes a change from
monstrous teeth.

Decorate the
Flump with a
scattering of
spots on the back
and legs.

A monster can have any
number of eyes you
want — and they don't
have to match!

Some tails hang down, some
stick up. The one thing they
never do in real life is stick
straight out behind. So what
does a monster's tail do?
You've got it!

What's a monster's
favorite meal?

Human beans!

(Of course, if they
see him coming,
they'll probably be
runner beans!)

Werewolf

Werewolves in old stories are scary, because they change shape so convincingly. Anyone might be a werewolf in human form! Modern versions often forget to lose the hair and teeth when they become human — the cartoon kind more than most!

Plan where the eyes will be.

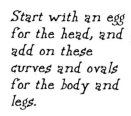

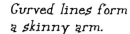

Start with an egg for the head, and add on these curves and ovals for the body and legs.

Even a hand can be built up with added ovals, which will form clutching fingers and thumb.

Curved lines form a skinny arm.

These oval shapes will give you the rough outline of your werewolf's shaggy mane.

I used to be a werewolf, but I'm all right nooooooow!

Start building up the face, feature by feature. Sketch small circles under the eyes to help build up the muzzle beyond the human shape.

Use eye shape to express the mood of your character. These round eyes create a comic look, where long narrow eyes would look more sinister.

A few short lines sketch in hair on the arms.

What big teeth you have, Grandmother! Remember to draw longer canine teeth at the corners of the mouth.

Head hair stretches down the back in a shaggy mane.

Tip fingers and thumbs with claws.

The contrast between the monstrous front part of the beast and the weedy little legs adds to the humor of the drawing.

Slugg

The common-or-garden slug is a mini-monster in the eyes of the squeamish — and of any gardener. You can build on this real-life creepy-crawly to create the monstrous Slugg, complete with horns, wings, and a toothy grin.

The head is an egg shape with two eyes on top.

Build up the body in three parts, overlapping the base of the shape that makes the head.

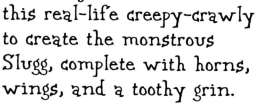

The small wing sprouts on a stalk from the middle of the back.

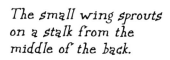

Start putting in details. Fringe the smile with teeth, add small horns below the eyes, and sketch in wing feathers. This is a weird one!

Shape the join between head and chest into the smooth curves of a long neck.

Ugliness is only skin-deep. Of course, some monsters have awfully thick skins!

Decorate the chest with a pattern of spots, and do the same down the back. If you make the spots different shapes — circles and ovals — they will look more interesting.

Draw in a single eyebrow floating above the head.

Have you ever seen odder-looking wings?

The tail curls upward, like a happy dog's.

Make the underneath of the Slugg wavy, rather than straight, to show how it ripples along the ground.

A shadow at the base of the neck helps to make the head look heavy and solid.

The Slugg isn't altogether a new invention. In ancient times it would have been classified as a Worm, or Wyrm, a kind of slimy legless dragon.

Ogre

The ogre is the nastiest kind of giant. He eats people but, luckily for the heroes who have to deal with ogres, he isn't usually very bright.

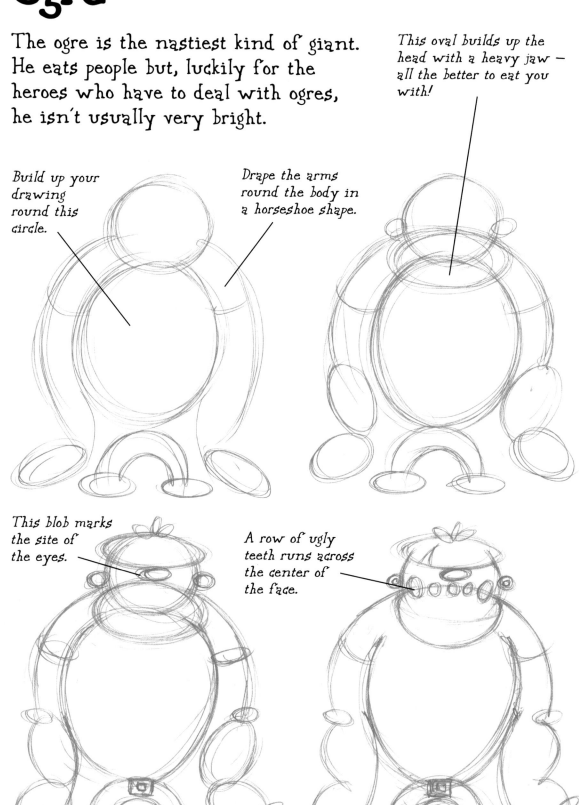

Build up your drawing round this circle.

Drape the arms round the body in a horseshoe shape.

This oval builds up the head with a heavy jaw — all the better to eat you with!

This blob marks the site of the eyes.

A row of ugly teeth runs across the center of the face.

Shape the hair, with a fringe.

Huge arms bulge with muscles and the knuckles trail on the ground.

Comical little legs end in short, round feet.

Cartoons exaggerate important features. So the dangerous bits — head, arms, and stomach (think about it!) — are huge, while the legs are the smallest part of the drawing.

This guy's mouth is watering. Get ready to run for it.

Keep clothes simple: trousers, T-shirt, and a single decorative touch, the belt buckle.

The hero said to the ogre, 'Your stomach is enormous. You should diet!'

And the ogre replied, 'Okay. What color?'

Blobb

Monsters don't have to be shapely — they can be as blobby as you like. Here's what happens when you start with a simple idea and add a few teeth and tentacles. The Blobb isn't a very scary monster — unless you imagine it the size of a house!

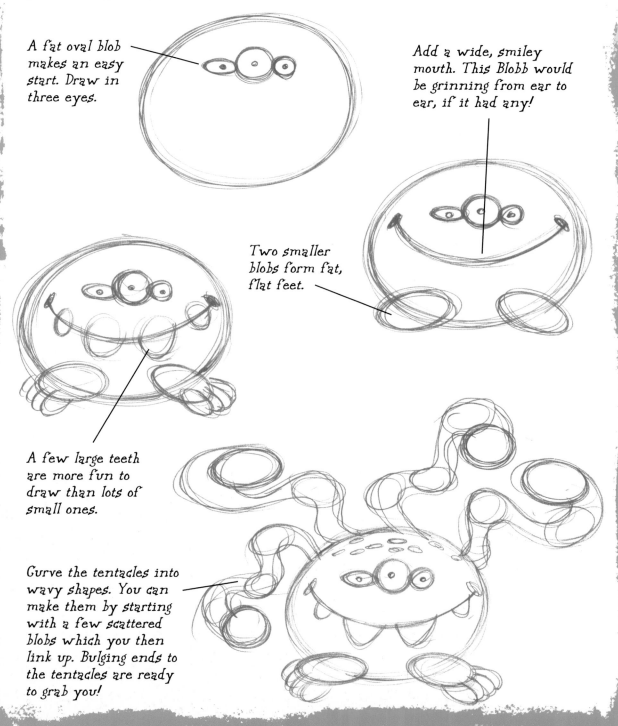

A fat oval blob makes an easy start. Draw in three eyes.

Add a wide, smiley mouth. This Blobb would be grinning from ear to ear, if it had any!

Two smaller blobs form fat, flat feet.

A few large teeth are more fun to draw than lots of small ones.

Curve the tentacles into wavy shapes. You can make them by starting with a few scattered blobs which you then link up. Bulging ends to the tentacles are ready to grab you!

Dapple the forehead with a few spots or splatters.

This monster's got no nose.

How does he smell?

Awful!

Small shadows behind the eyes give them depth.

Curving shadows within the tentacles help to make them look solid.

Is he waving hello, or should you be waving goodbye?

Frankenstein's Monster

Frankenstein was so keen on Do-It-Yourself that he built his own monster out of bits and pieces. But it didn't work very well! And, as you can see, he wasn't too good at needlework. His stitches had to be reinforced with bolts.

Sketch out the rough shape with curved lines.

Curved lines establish a heavy jaw and mouth

Two ovals help to form built-up boots.

Draw in the collar and buttons, and the whole jacket begins to take shape.

Make the hands enormous. The monster is made out of bits of different people, and they don't fit together very well. It makes you wonder why Frankenstein didn't wait to collect a matching set of pieces.

Draw in a line of stitches round the neck, and start drawing the metal nuts and bolts on either side.

Small close-set eyes stare straight ahead from under a single eyebrow.

Try drawing the shading as a bold zig-zag pattern.

The legs are braced apart, showing that it is an effort for this monster to walk.

Where does frankenstein keep his money?

In an organ bank!

Fluff

Have you ever wondered about those bits of fluff under the bed? Supposing they were alive, what would they look like? Here's one idea. Fluff is only small, but are you sure you want him lurking under your bed? Perhaps it's time to clean!

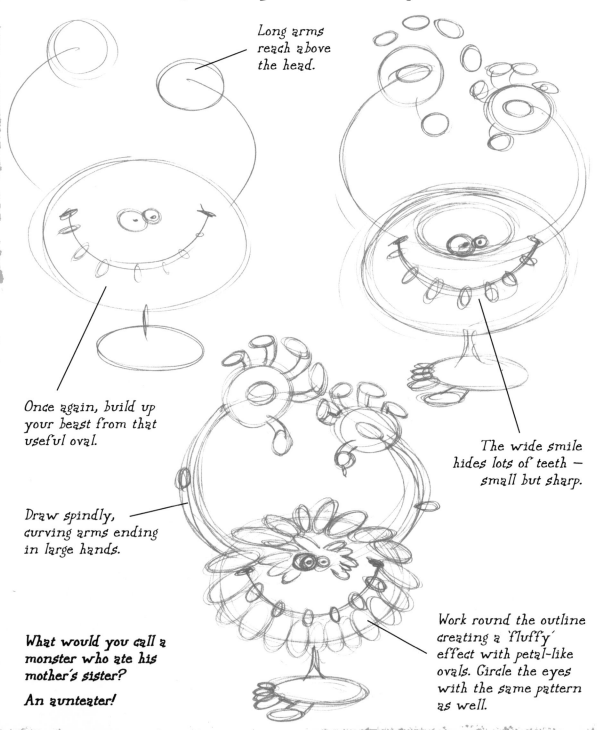

Long arms reach above the head.

Once again, build up your beast from that useful oval.

Draw spindly, curving arms ending in large hands.

The wide smile hides lots of teeth — small but sharp.

Work round the outline creating a 'fluffy' effect with petal-like ovals. Circle the eyes with the same pattern as well.

What would you call a monster who ate his mother's sister?

An aunteater!

The fingers are curved with sharp claws, ready to grab!

Fluff isn't a great walker: he's only got one foot. Make the toes comically irregular, with a long big toe and smaller toes to the side.

A few little lumps and bumps on the arms add to the spiky effect.

Knowing eyes and a toothy smirk make it clear that he may be fluffy, but he isn't cuddly.

Minion

Some monsters live in spooky castles, where it is essential that they have at least one creepy servant. That's Minion's job. He's a sort of butler, who is employed by his monster master to bow guests in, though perhaps not out again.

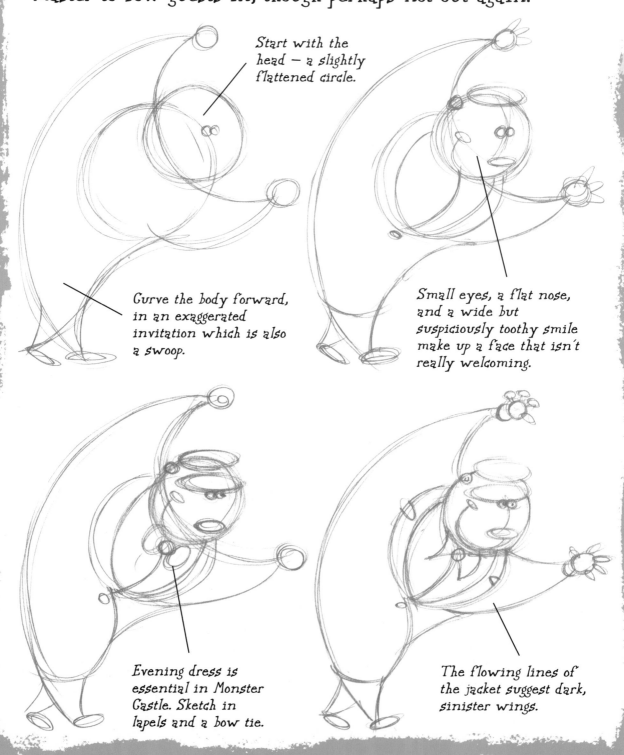

Start with the head — a slightly flattened circle.

Curve the body forward, in an exaggerated invitation which is also a swoop.

Small eyes, a flat nose, and a wide but suspiciously toothy smile make up a face that isn't really welcoming.

Evening dress is essential in Monster Castle. Sketch in lapels and a bow tie.

The flowing lines of the jacket suggest dark, sinister wings.

The single eyebrow forms a curve that bulges out above the lower face.

Continue the body curve down the legs, ending in tiny feet.

Finish drawing the face with a flattened nose, tiny eyes, and a mouth positively frilled with teeth.

Contrast the smooth perfection of Minion's costume with the cragginess of his face.

Did you hear about the vegetarian monster?

He would only eat Swedes. . .and the occasional Norwegian!

There is no need to draw Minion's shadow — his kind don't have them.

Harpy

The Harpy is a monster from ancient Greece who comes to punish wicked behavior. Part woman, part vulture, filthy and smelly, she specializes in snatching sinners' dinners from their tables.

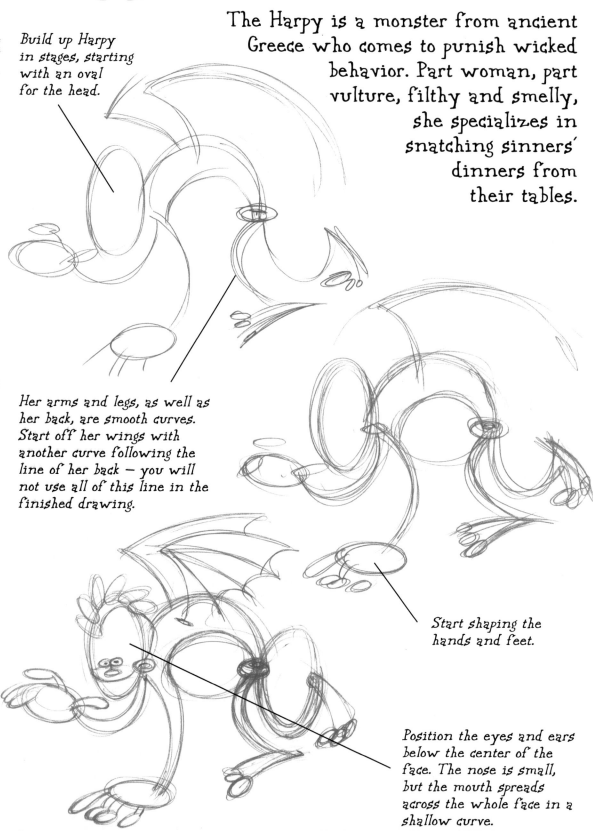

Build up Harpy in stages, starting with an oval for the head.

Her arms and legs, as well as her back, are smooth curves. Start off her wings with another curve following the line of her back — you will not use all of this line in the finished drawing.

Start shaping the hands and feet.

Position the eyes and ears below the center of the face. The nose is small, but the mouth spreads across the whole face in a shallow curve.

These are bat wings rather than bird wings, with spokes and folds like an umbrella.

The body is a sinuous, slender arch. Draw an exaggerated belt where the body joins the legs, to help form a comically skimpy pair of pants.

Finish off the head with a jagged crest of hair.

Two sharp fangs hang down from the mouth like a vampire's — all the better to eat your dinner with!

C (Sea) Monster

You can make an amusing monster out of any letter of the alphabet: you might find this one in the ocean. In the days when books were written by hand, instead of being printed, some writers used to decorate their capital letters with strange twisted beasts or people. Now it's your turn!

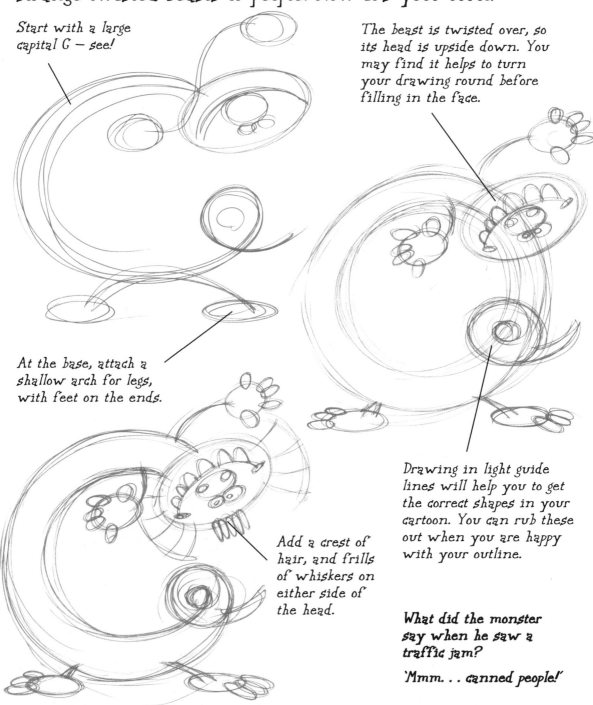

Start with a large capital C — see!

The beast is twisted over, so its head is upside down. You may find it helps to turn your drawing round before filling in the face.

At the base, attach a shallow arch for legs, with feet on the ends.

Add a crest of hair, and frills of whiskers on either side of the head.

Drawing in light guide lines will help you to get the correct shapes in your cartoon. You can rub these out when you are happy with your outline.

What did the monster say when he saw a traffic jam?

'Mmm. . . canned people!'

Keep the arms small, so you don't obscure your 'G' shape.

This is a rather jolly monster. Big eyes and a zany grin give him a happy expression. The hands echo the shape of the head.

The end of the 'G' flows quite naturally into a coiled tail.

When you ink in your outlines, you can add details like whisker spots on his cheeks. A zig-zag pattern down his back and across his forehead add to the overall effect.

When you design an alphabet monster, it's important not to lose the shape of the letter. You can use monsters like this to decorate the words on party invitations and posters.

Godzilla

This giant radioactive dinosaur is a hero of the Japanese movie industry. In early movies, he is a threat to humankind. In later appearances he is on our side, and saves the human race from a whole host of other monsters.

Godzilla went on a cruise. He went to the restaurant for dinner, and the waiter asked if he would like to see the menu.

'No,' he replied, 'just bring me the passenger list!'

Start with this upturned crescent for the body. Add a big blunt head, marking the position of the eyes.

Draw a second oval overlapping the lower half of the head to help form the mouth.

Draw an arch for legs, and large rounded feet on the ends of them.

Start to form the toes using small oval shapes.

Sketch in a row of scaley plates down the back, and add tiny arms.

Draw in eyes and nostrils, and shape the open mouth with its row of teeth.

See how the arch you drew for the legs helps you to position them correctly.

Make the hands small and dainty on their tiny arms.

Drawing the nostrils like this gives them a raised appearance. Godzilla smells something good!

With those strong legs, feeble hands, and big, broad head, Godzilla is clearly based on the famous Tyrannosaurus.

Fishface

Monsters can be as monstrous as you like. You can take bits and pieces from all sorts of ideas and mix them together. What happens if you combine a big round head, human arms, and a fish's tail? Let's put them together and see!

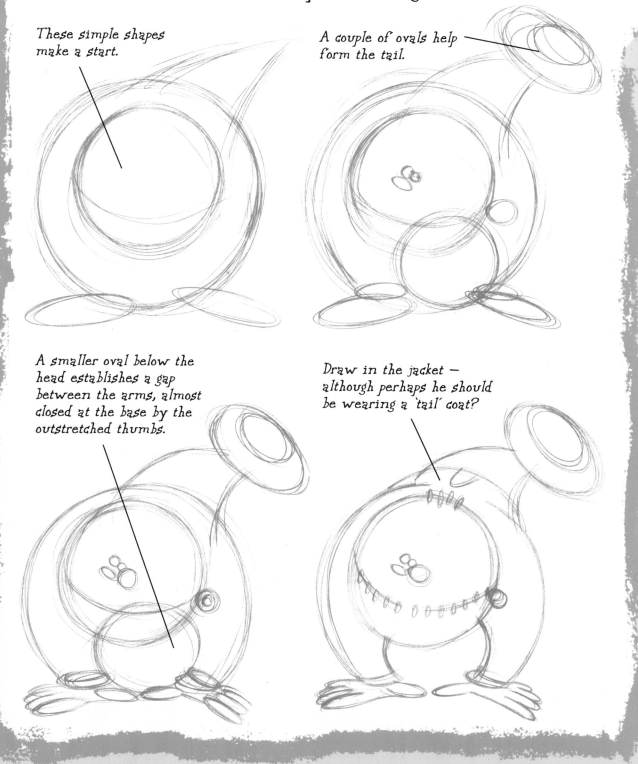

These simple shapes make a start.

A couple of ovals help form the tail.

A smaller oval below the head establishes a gap between the arms, almost closed at the base by the outstretched thumbs.

Draw in the jacket — although perhaps he should be wearing a 'tail' coat?

He has tiny eyes and
a button nose.

Sketch in a sprinkling
of scales on the tail.

Small teeth are more
comical than
threatening.

The hands are spread out to take
his weight. Fishface has to walk
on his hands, since he hasn't
any legs!

You could leave Fishface
bald, but be generous
and give him a few
spiky hairs.

Ink in your cartoon
and color Fishface in
suitably watery tones.

When is the only day
you can play a trick on
a monster?

April Ghoul's Day!

Golem

A golem is a robot man made out of clay by a sorcerer. He is brought to life by special words written on a paper tucked inside his head. Making pottery is not a skill practiced by many sorcerers, so golems are rarely as good-looking as you or me.

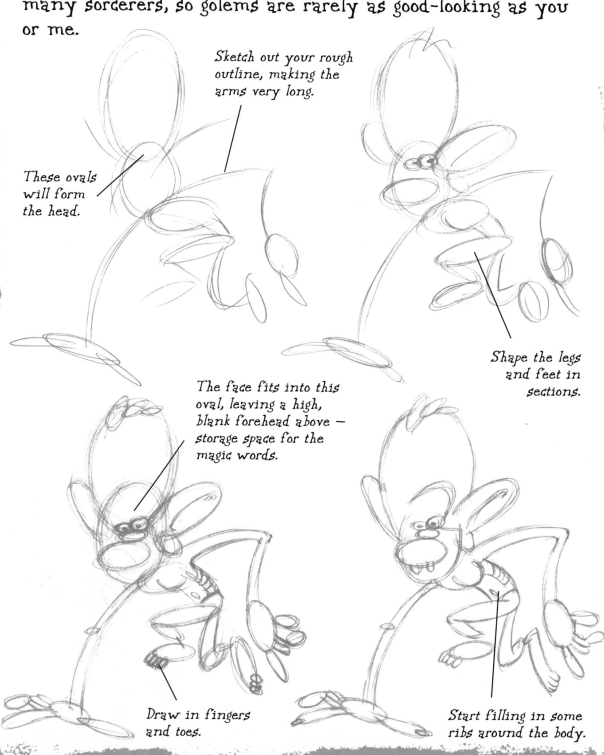

These ovals will form the head.

Sketch out your rough outline, making the arms very long.

Shape the legs and feet in sections.

The face fits into this oval, leaving a high, blank forehead above — storage space for the magic words.

Draw in fingers and toes.

Start filling in some ribs around the body.

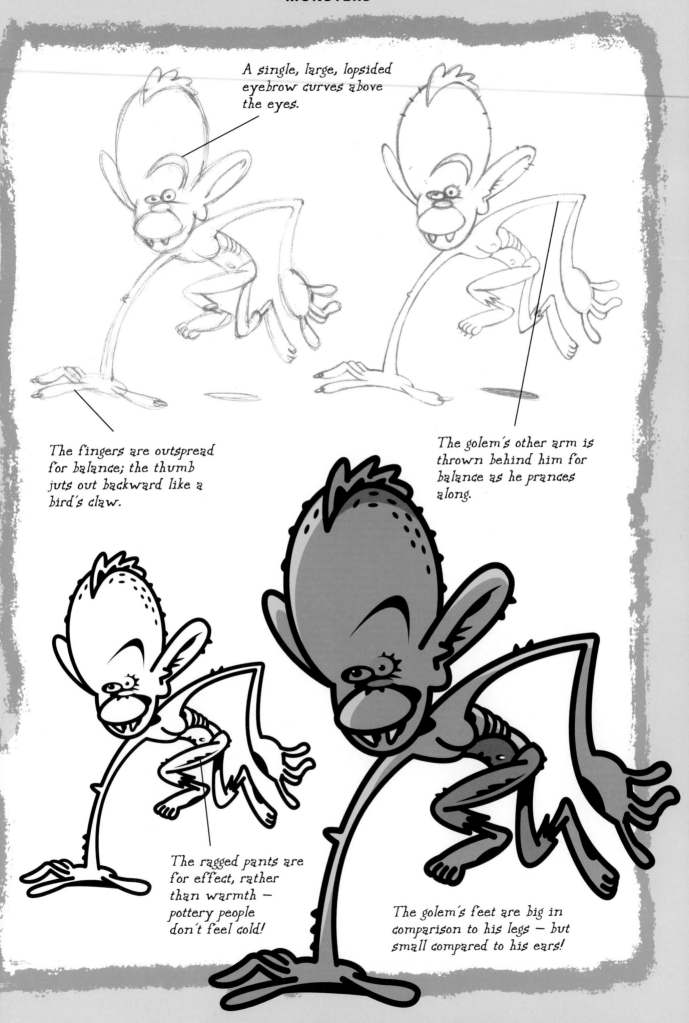

A single, large, lopsided eyebrow curves above the eyes.

The fingers are outspread for balance; the thumb juts out backward like a bird's claw.

The golem's other arm is thrown behind him for balance as he prances along.

The ragged pants are for effect, rather than warmth — pottery people don't feel cold!

The golem's feet are big in comparison to his legs — but small compared to his ears!

Sun With Hat On

To scientists, the Sun is a ball of burning gas. Artists often prefer to depict it as a smiling golden face surrounded by bright rays. All we need to do is dress this up a little, with hat and gloves, to create a jolly cartoon Sun.

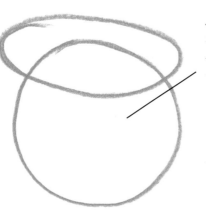

Start with the round face, crowned by a rough oval for the hat brim.

Hat and brim together are the same height as the whole face.

Draw in the hatband.

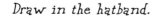

In cartoons, hands are often drawn with only three fingers (and a thumb).

Little flames fringe the edges to form the Sun's rays — and, at the same time, make a beard to finish off the face.

Ignore the lower curve of the hat when drawing the face — this was just a guideline to help you position the hat brim.

Ink in the outlines of the hat with flowing curves. The hand on the brim is raising the hat in greeting.

Below the mouth, draw a jolly double chin.

For a welcoming smile, the mouth curves up in the center as well as at the corners.

In the words of the old song: 'The sun has got his hat on — hip, hip, hip, hooray!'

I got up at dawn this morning to see the sunrise.

Well, you couldn't have picked a better time!

Meteorite

A meteorite is a piece of rock that comes blasting out of space. If it hits Earth, it lands with a real bang. Most meteorites miss Earth, but the one in this drawing has every intention of hitting something — or somebody!

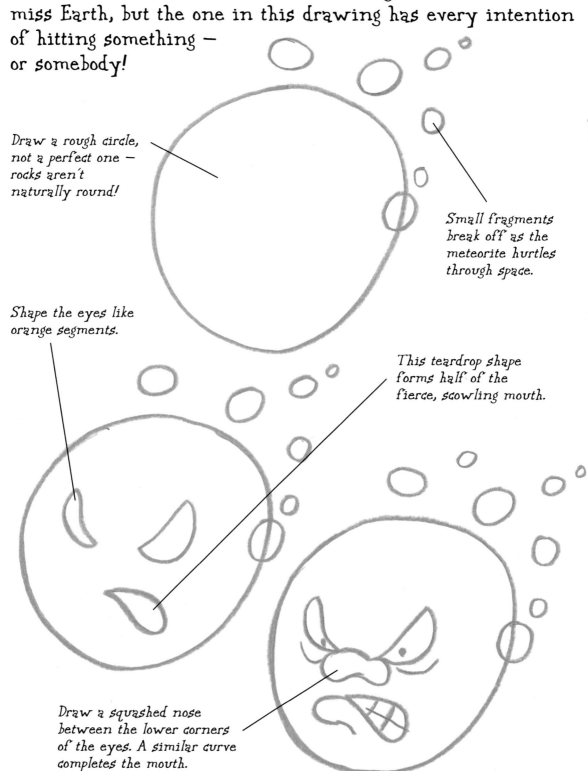

Draw a rough circle, not a perfect one — rocks aren't naturally round!

Small fragments break off as the meteorite hurtles through space.

Shape the eyes like orange segments.

This teardrop shape forms half of the fierce, scowling mouth.

Draw a squashed nose between the lower corners of the eyes. A similar curve completes the mouth.

These curves suggest heavy eyebrows.

As you ink in the features, start adding little dots and streaks to create the rough texture of rock.

Use wavy lines and curves, not sharp zig-zags, to make the outline rough and lumpy.

Teeth can be suggested quite easily with straight lines.

'Where should I park the rocket, man?'

'Wherever you see a space, man.'

Flying Saucer

Many people believe that 'Unidentified Flying Objects' seen in the skies are alien spacecraft. They got their nickname of 'flying saucers' in 1947, when an American described them as skipping through the air 'like saucers over water.'

A long flat oval forms the shape of a saucer seen at an oblique angle.

Add a curved line over the top to give the saucer depth. You can see from this shape how some people have managed to fake 'flying saucer' photos using ordinary buttons or lampshades!

Add a smaller oval below, for the base. In movies, this section is often shown opening up to 'beam up' objects from Earth into the craft.

Crown the structure with a domed top, and your spacecraft is almost complete.

A row of small, square portholes enables the aliens to look down on Earth.

Dividing the top part into curved sections helps to make it look like the control center of the spinning craft.

Take care, when inking in, to keep your curves smooth and flowing. The only straight lines are the edges of the portholes.

What did the astronaut spot in the kitchen?

An Unidentified Frying Object.

Space Shuttle

The Space Shuttle, first launched in 1981, looks a bit like a cross between a jet plane and a rocket. It can make repeated journeys into space and back again — unlike earlier space rockets, that made one trip and then burned up and were destroyed.

Start with this long sausage shape, a bit narrower at this end.

On the side of this shape, add a short, fat wing.

This wing is farther away, so you can't see quite as much of it.

Add the viewing windows of the flight deck — which will double as eyes when you give the Shuttle a face.

Draw the tall tail fin, and a blob at the back for the engines.

In this drawing, the pointed nose cone of the Shuttle is rounded off, to make it look more like a smiling face.

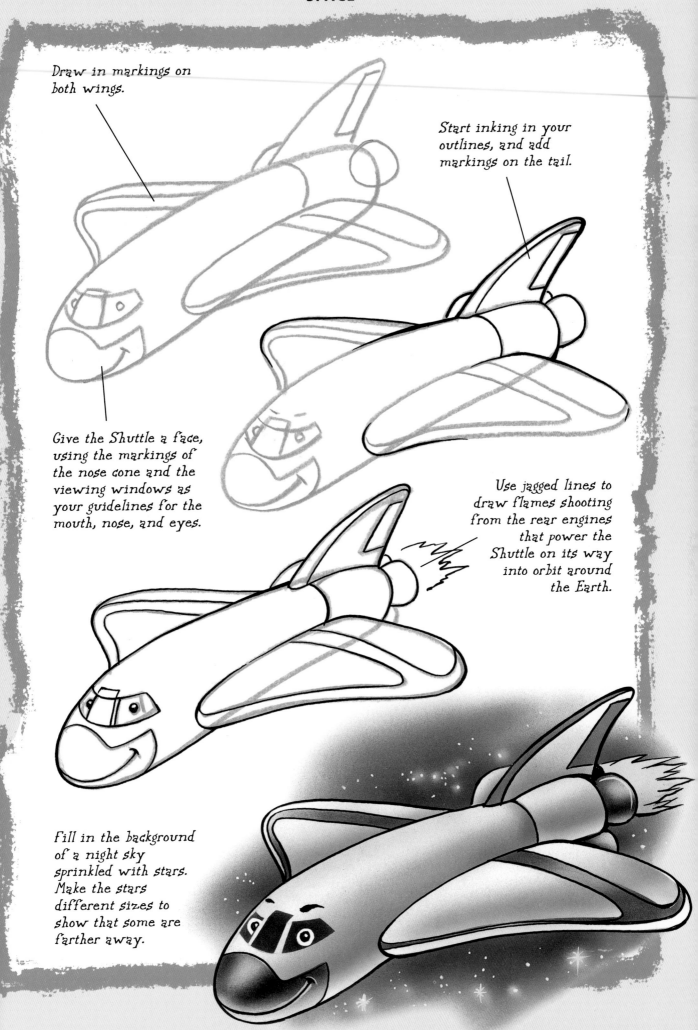

Draw in markings on both wings.

Start inking in your outlines, and add markings on the tail.

Give the Shuttle a face, using the markings of the nose cone and the viewing windows as your guidelines for the mouth, nose, and eyes.

Use jagged lines to draw flames shooting from the rear engines that power the Shuttle on its way into orbit around the Earth.

Fill in the background of a night sky sprinkled with stars. Make the stars different sizes to show that some are farther away.

Saturn

Nine planets (including Earth) orbit the Sun. Everybody recognizes Saturn, because of its famous rings. Actually, three other planets have rings too — but nobody remembers that, because Saturn's are so much more spectacular.

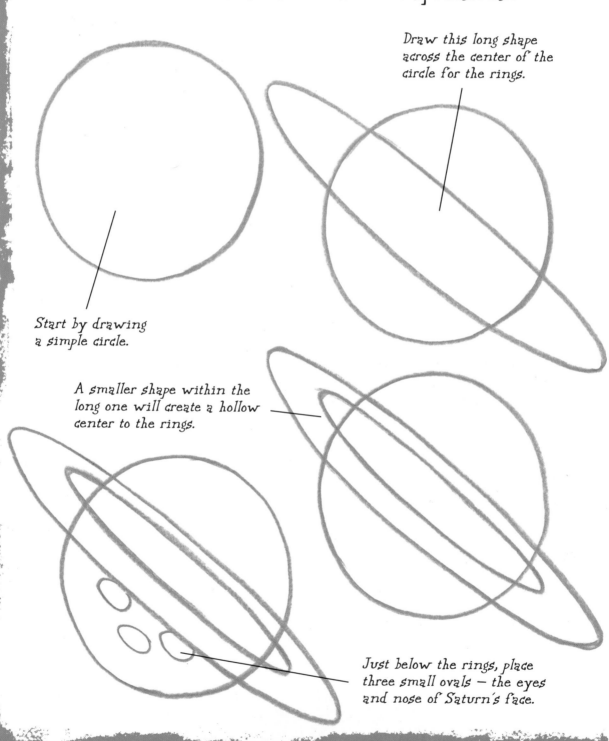

Draw this long shape across the center of the circle for the rings.

Start by drawing a simple circle.

A smaller shape within the long one will create a hollow center to the rings.

Just below the rings, place three small ovals — the eyes and nose of Saturn's face.

Now you can draw the whole face. Make the features big enough to occupy all the space below the rings.

Don't ink in the upper part of the rings, which will be hidden behind Saturn's face. You can rub out these pencil guidelines later.

Smile lines around the eyes help to give the face a kindly expression. A little chin juts out at the bottom.

Saturn's many shimmering rings, made up of ice and dust, are simplified here into a single ring. A star-filled night sky behind completes the heavenly scene.

Exploding Rocket

Space rockets aren't meant to explode. But the fireworks of the same name certainly are. If you put the two ideas together, you can draw a truly spectacular rocket that really does go off with a bang.

Set this rounded shape at the top, so that the two pieces together look like a straight finger with a fingernail at the end.

This long cylindrical shape forms the body of the rocket.

Draw a jagged line about a third of the way down, to mark where the top of the rocket is breaking away from the bottom in the explosion.

In the center, draw a cloud of smoke, with little puffs of smoke to either side. Below this, another jagged line shows where the base of the rocket has broken off.

Add a rounded tail fin on either side of the base.

Add a third tail fin. It looks a different shape because of the angle at which we are looking at it.

Scatter small triangular fragments through the cloud of smoke.

A few small curves within the cloud give it greater depth.

These round shapes form the rocket's engines.

Remember to rub out these guidelines. This part of the rocket has disappeared.

Short, straight 'speed lines' between the shattered rocket and the smoke give the impression of movement.

What do you get if you cross a round black hat with a rocket?

A very fast bowler.

Small Robot

Robots can boldly go where humans can't. This makes them very useful in space, so movies about space travel often feature walking, talking robots. Small robots tend to look rather appealing to us, as if we think of them as cute pets.

The head is almost as big as the squat, chunky body.

Draw the jointed arms using two ovals for each.

Three little curves on top of the head mimic hair.

The feet form a wide base, so the robot will not topple over easily.

These two shape form pincer 'hands.'

Small rectangles for eyes, and straight lines for eyebrows and mouth, make this a mechanical face, not a human one.

Use straight lines to draw in the body panels.

Draw big bolts at the joints of the arms where sections overlap.

Why are robots never afraid?

Because they have nerves of steel.

Crescent Moon

The Moon is much more than just a lump of rock in the sky. Its silvery light and changing shape make it seem magical. Some people see a face in its surface: the Man in the Moon. On the other hand, others see a rabbit there instead!

Draw your Moon, with the bulge of a face and nose just above the center.

Draw this circle (the spaceman's head) about its own diameter away from the Moon.

How can you tell that the Moon is pleased to see you?

The Moon beams.

Two more ovals complete his body. Add arms with big gloved hands, and the far leg. A circle within the head shape gives you the face within the clear helmet.

These four small ovals form the lower part of the spaceman's body, and his large boots.

Just above the Moon's nose, draw a large oval eye, nearly as big as the nose.

Sketch in the spaceman's face, giving him a big, friendly grin.

Finish drawing the Moon's face. When you draw in the eye, place the pupil quite low down so that the Moon is looking downward, directly at his visitor.

Ink in your outlines. Make sure you have the spaceman's face looking up at the Moon. All those ovals you used to draw his body help to create the shape of his bouncy spacesuit now.

When you color in your drawing, use shading to give a rounded look to the sections of the spacesuit. And add some twinkling stars in the background.

Spacecraft

The age of space exploration has begun — but there are still more spacecraft to be seen in the cinemas than in the skies. This gives you a lot of freedom when it comes to designing your own spacecraft — try this one for a start.

Start with this long oval.

Draw two smaller shapes on either side. These are the boosters, to provide extra power and speed. Be sure to make the one on the left smaller, because it is farther away.

Draw in the viewing window of the flight deck near the front. It is shaped rather like an orange segment. Then add two egg shapes at the back of the craft for the rear engines.

Link up the boosters to the main body of the craft with two broad, wing-like sections. Draw a broad stripe across the back, and start rounding off the curves of the rear engines.

Add a row of small square portholes along the side.

Divide up the front viewing window into three unequal sections.

The booster engines each consist of several sections, which you can sketch in a bit at a time.

What do you get if you cross a miserable man with a spaceship?

A moan rocket!

Shape the rear engines so that they fit on to the rear of the craft.

Behind the 'wing,' sketch in the surface of a planet stretching below the spacecraft. Later you can paint in craters on the planet's surface.

Merry Martian

People can't agree on whether aliens exist somewhere out in space, let alone what they look like if they do! This means you can have fun designing your own aliens. You can make them any shape you like — and nobody can prove you're wrong!

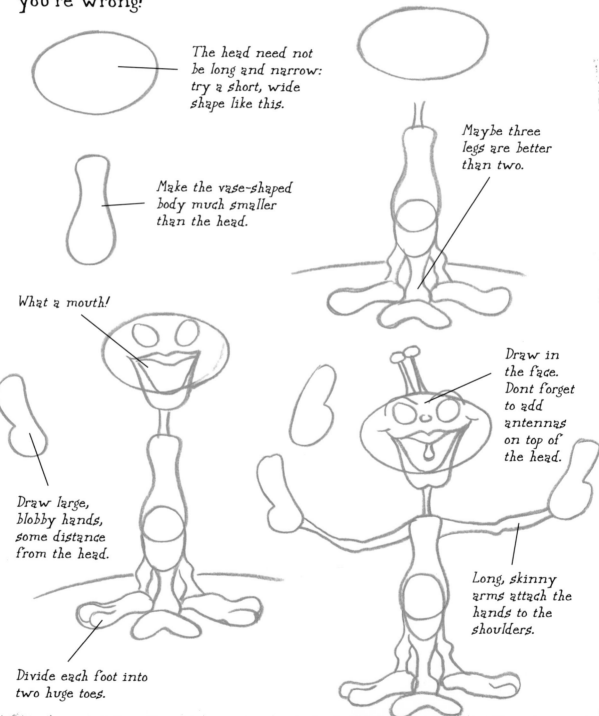

The head need not be long and narrow: try a short, wide shape like this.

Make the vase-shaped body much smaller than the head.

Maybe three legs are better than two.

What a mouth!

Draw in the face. Dont forget to add antennas on top of the head.

Draw large, blobby hands, some distance from the head.

Long, skinny arms attach the hands to the shoulders.

Divide each foot into two huge toes.

Exaggerate the size of the big lower lip.

Give the hands long, knobbly fingers.

The top of the head is shaped around the big eyes. Who needs a forehead when you can have antennas instead?

Outstretched arms and a big smile suggest a welcome. 'Take me to your leader.'

Although clearly an alien, this Martian is based on a human model. But where could you buy three shoes to fit him?

Rocket Rider

A cartoonist can draw the impossible. You may be inspired to reverse the way things usually are. An astronaut travels inside a large rocket. Turn this round and imagine him riding on the outside of a small rocket. Not very comfortable — but fun to draw!

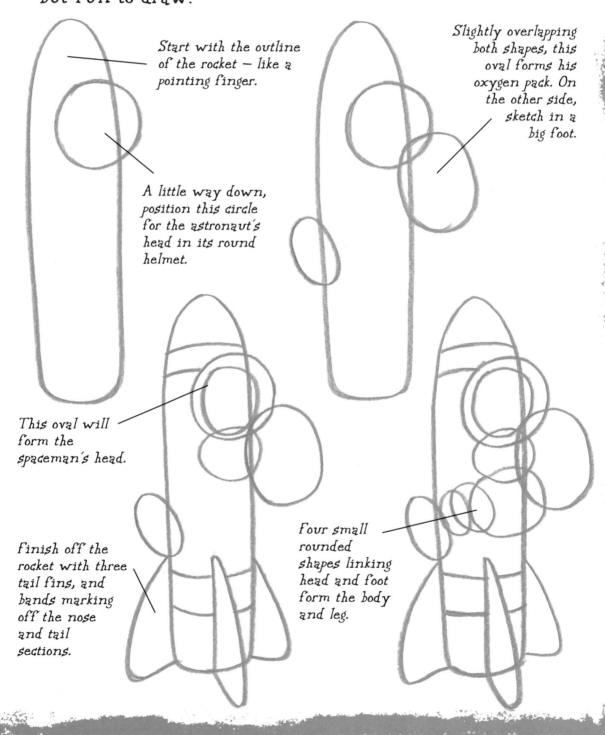

Start with the outline of the rocket — like a pointing finger.

A little way down, position this circle for the astronaut's head in its round helmet.

Slightly overlapping both shapes, this oval forms his oxygen pack. On the other side, sketch in a big foot.

This oval will form the spaceman's head.

Finish off the rocket with three tail fins, and bands marking off the nose and tail sections.

Four small rounded shapes linking head and foot form the body and leg.

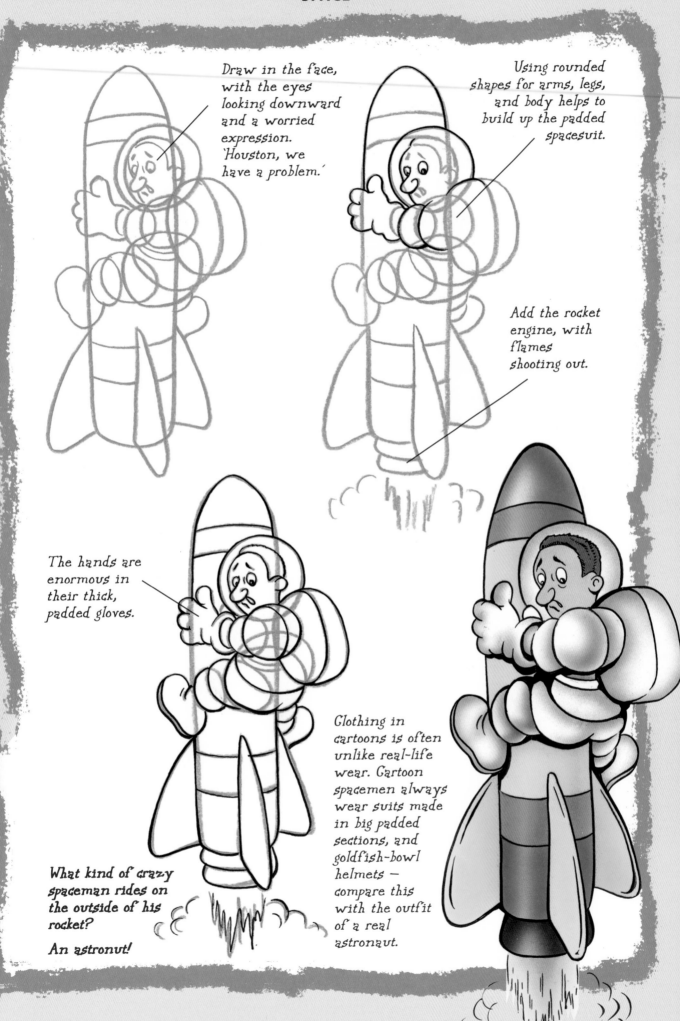

Draw in the face, with the eyes looking downward and a worried expression. 'Houston, we have a problem.'

Using rounded shapes for arms, legs, and body helps to build up the padded spacesuit.

Add the rocket engine, with flames shooting out.

The hands are enormous in their thick, padded gloves.

Clothing in cartoons is often unlike real-life wear. Cartoon spacemen always wear suits made in big padded sections, and goldfish-bowl helmets — compare this with the outfit of a real astronaut.

What kind of crazy spaceman rides on the outside of his rocket?

An astronut!

Moon-Walking

When the first astronaut took 'one giant step for mankind' on the surface of the Moon, this isn't quite what he meant! Swapping round the sizes of Moon and astronaut produces a great comic effect. Giving the Moon a face helps, too!

Start with a good big circle for the Moon.

Two small overlapping circles form the astronaut's head and body.

Give the Moon eyes and a smiling mouth.

Finish off the astronaut. Placing his arms outstretched shows that he is having to work at keeping his balance on the Moon.

Keep the face simple.

The astronaut has planted a flag.

Add some detail to the Moon's facial features. Those are craters, not freckles!

The Moon's eyes are turned upward to see who is dancing on his head. A wide smile welcomes the Earthling.

Small crescents depict craters on the Moon's surface.

Make the Moon's outline a little uneven, to represent the rough surface.

Alien and Spaceman

The contrast between two different figures — here an alien and a spaceman — can be brought out by drawing them in the same pose. Here the two stand facing one another, communicating in sign language — thumbs up!

Five ovals, of varying shapes and sizes, start you off. Be careful to get the proportions right.

Smaller ovals are used to form the man's arms, feet, and oxygen tank, and the alien's feet — all three of them. The alien's neck links up with his head by way of another oval.

Another, interlinked curve shapes the spaceman's arm in its thick, padded sleeve, and a final oval forms his hand.

The alien's skinny, bendy legs and arms match his tube-like neck, and contrast with the bulky limbs of the spaceman in his spacesuit.

Now you can draw in features. Both figures have similar long noses and friendly smiles, but you can have fun making the eyes very different. The alien's eyes are placed high and mounted on stalks

Both characters have simple hands, and hold their thumbs up in the same way.

Your curved guidelines help shape padded sleeves. Use similar curves to form the legs.

Your alien can be any color you like — ours is bright red, but you could choose green or blue.

What do you do if you see a spaceman?

Park your car in it, man.

Dancing Alien

We usually imagine aliens as being about the same size as us. (It makes it easier to fit actors into alien costumes for movies!) But there's no reason why they should be. This alien could fit into your hand — but he is having much more fun dancing on a spaceman's helmet.

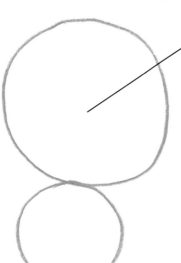

Starting couldn't be easier: just draw two circles, one bigger than the other.

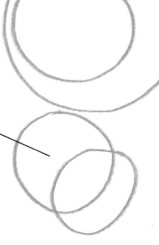

Two more large shapes establish the spaceman's shoulder and arm. Draw another circle for his head within his helmet.

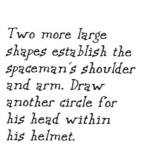

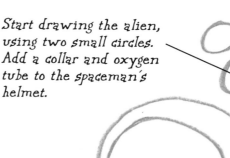

Start drawing the alien, using two small circles. Add a collar and oxygen tube to the spaceman's helmet.

Complete the arm and hand with two more circles. Behind the shoulder, a rounded oblong forms the spaceman's oxygen tank.

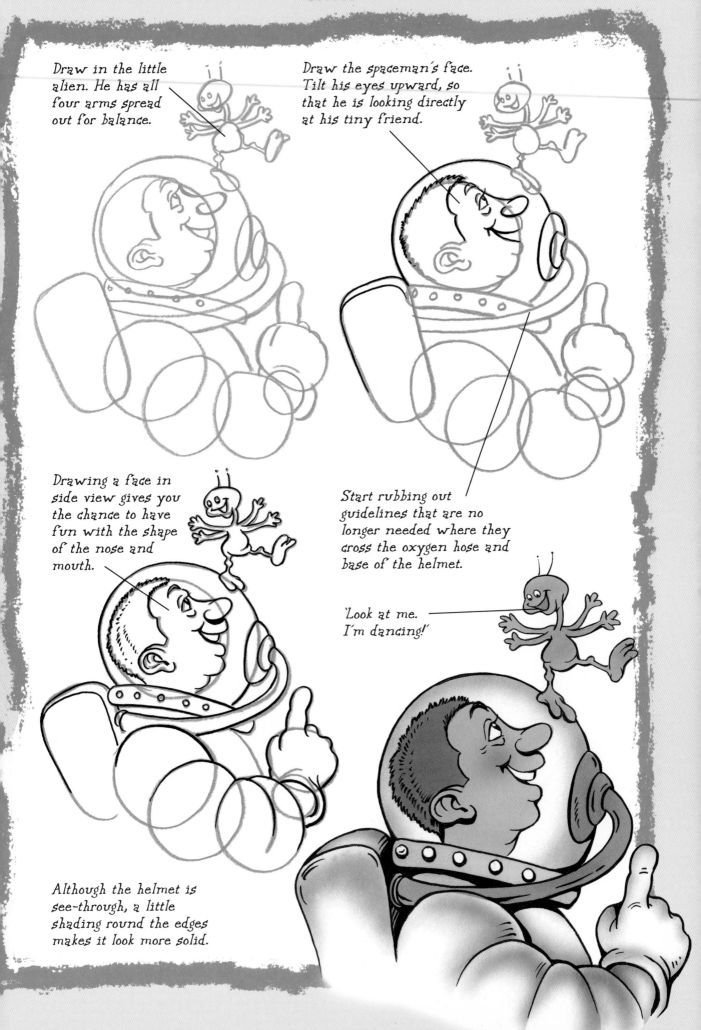

Draw in the little alien. He has all four arms spread out for balance.

Draw the spaceman's face. Tilt his eyes upward, so that he is looking directly at his tiny friend.

Drawing a face in side view gives you the chance to have fun with the shape of the nose and mouth.

Start rubbing out guidelines that are no longer needed where they cross the oxygen hose and base of the helmet.

'Look at me. I'm dancing!'

Although the helmet is see-through, a little shading round the edges makes it look more solid.

Large Robot

If small robots are usually cute or comical (in sci-fi movies at least), big robots are usually more like humans in their shape. In fact, some of them look quite like walking suits of armor. They may be friendly or sinister, depending on your taste. This one looks harmless!

Start with a circle for the head...

...and a larger oval for the upper part of the body.

An oval forms the lower part of the body. The whole drawing is made up of rounded sections, linked together like the pop-on beads of a necklace.

Add two more sections to each arm.

Smaller ovals form the shoulder of each arm.

The first leg joint is nearly as big as the lower part of the body.

The lower leg joint is as long as the upper part of the body.

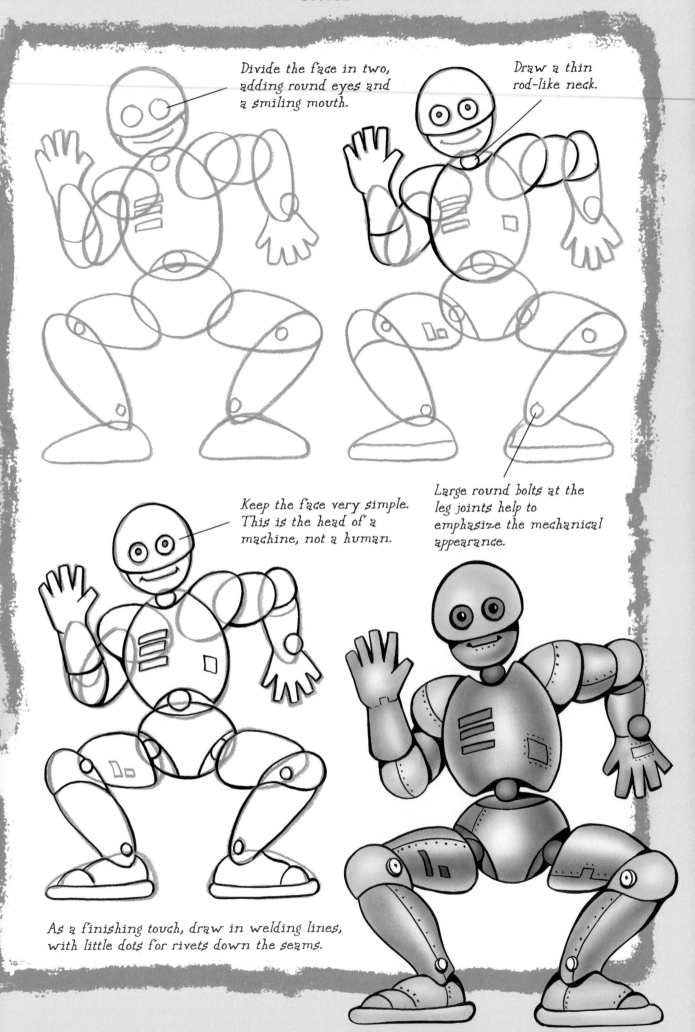

Divide the face in two, adding round eyes and a smiling mouth.

Draw a thin rod-like neck.

Large round bolts at the leg joints help to emphasize the mechanical appearance.

Keep the face very simple. This is the head of a machine, not a human.

As a finishing touch, draw in welding lines, with little dots for rivets down the seams.

Two-headed Alien

There's no reason why an alien should have the same number of heads as humans. Two heads are supposed to be better than one! That may be true when the two heads manage to agree, but this guy seems to be having problems!

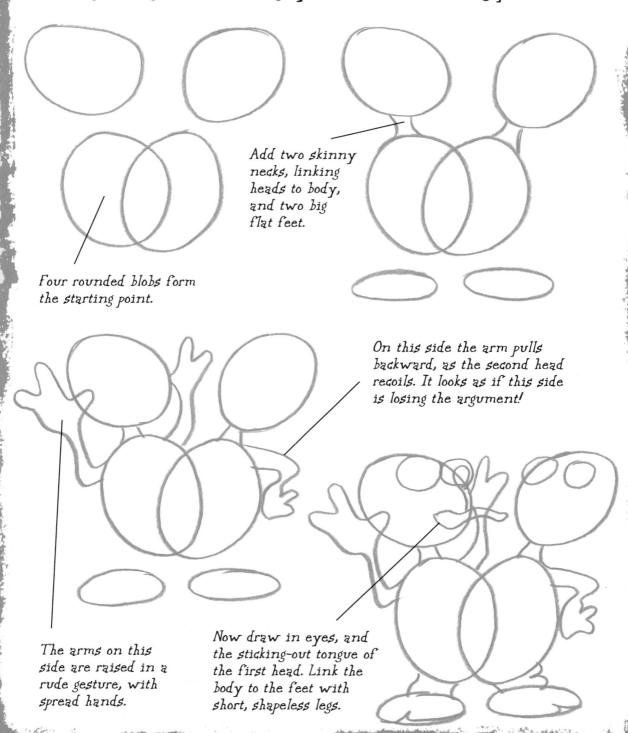

Four rounded blobs form the starting point.

Add two skinny necks, linking heads to body, and two big flat feet.

On this side the arm pulls backward, as the second head recoils. It looks as if this side is losing the argument!

The arms on this side are raised in a rude gesture, with spread hands.

Now draw in eyes, and the sticking-out tongue of the first head. Link the body to the feet with short, shapeless legs.

Finish drawing the faces. Small changes to the original guidelines for the heads will enable you to bulge out cheeks and narrow chins, making the heads more expressive.

The expression in the eyes tells the story.

The guidelines where the two original body shapes overlap are no longer needed. Let the two bodies merge into one lumpy form.

The shape of the hands is less important than the gestures they are making. The hands themselves can be quite roughly drawn.

Why does an alien always buy clothes at a ridiculous price?

Because he has to buy them for an absurd figure.

What did the alien say to the librarian?

Take me to your reader!

Teacher

One way of getting across a sense of character is to concentrate on the head. Making it much bigger than the body emphasizes the expression, as in the case of this stern teacher.

This drawing is made up of strict, straight lines. Start with these two boxes.

More straight lines build up the body and legs and mark out the blackboard. Start shaping the head by cutting off the corners.

Two curving lines across the face establish the site of eyebrows and mustache. Take care with these, for they form the basis of the expression.

Shape the trousers, and add tiny feet. Use short lines to pinch in the body at the waist

Draw the small arms and hands, and start adding detail to the jacket. Use the curve of the mustache to help shape the large nose.

Sketch in the eyeglasses and the rest of the face. The eyes peer over the top of the eyeglasses to give the class that piercing look we all know so well.

Drawing the body leaning toward the blackboard makes a more interesting picture than if the body were standing stiffly upright.

Ink in the eyebrows, lowered over the eyes in a frown, and the stern mustache. Frown lines beside the mouth add to the expression.

One foot is seen sideways on, but the other is turned toward the viewer, and therefore looks shorter.

Did you hear about the cross-eyed teacher?

He couldn't control his pupils!

Bully Boy

A caricature can express your opinion of someone. The bully thinks his physical strength makes him important. But by drawing him with a huge head on a small body, you can make his mean expression more significant than his muscles.

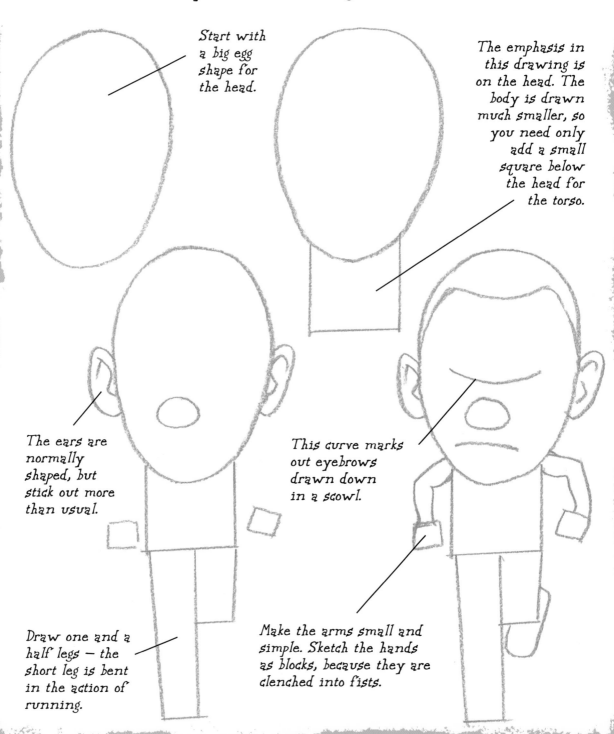

Start with a big egg shape for the head.

The emphasis in this drawing is on the head. The body is drawn much smaller, so you need only add a small square below the head for the torso.

The ears are normally shaped, but stick out more than usual.

This curve marks out eyebrows drawn down in a scowl.

Draw one and a half legs — the short leg is bent in the action of running.

Make the arms small and simple. Sketch the hands as blocks, because they are clenched into fists.

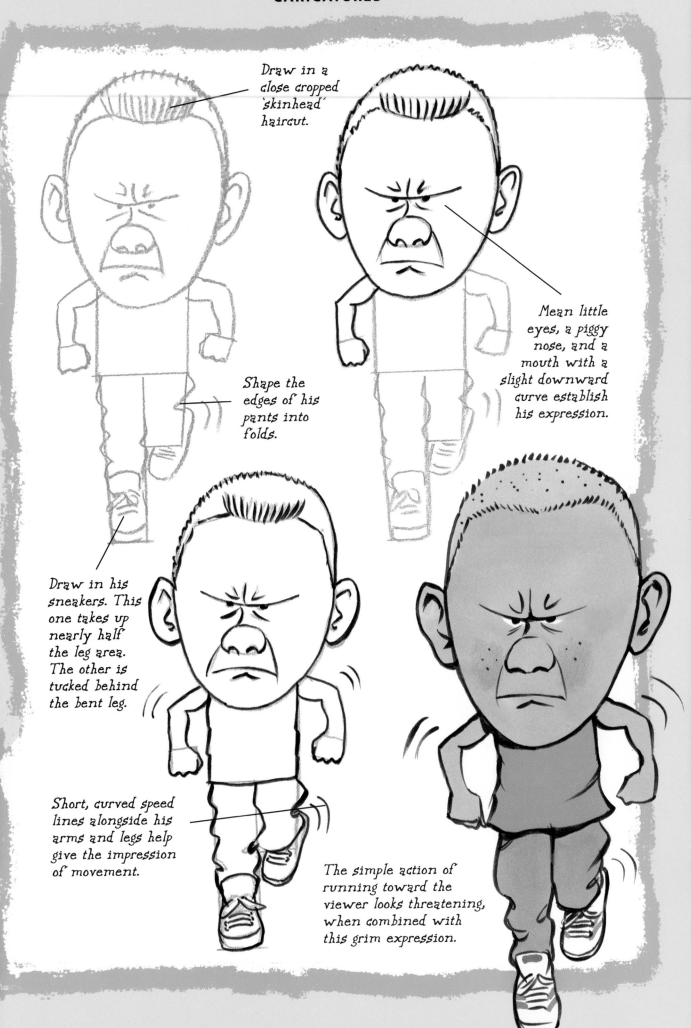

Draw in a close cropped 'skinhead' haircut.

Mean little eyes, a piggy nose, and a mouth with a slight downward curve establish his expression.

Shape the edges of his pants into folds.

Draw in his sneakers. This one takes up nearly half the leg area. The other is tucked behind the bent leg.

Short, curved speed lines alongside his arms and legs help give the impression of movement.

The simple action of running toward the viewer looks threatening, when combined with this grim expression.

Girl Scout Leader

Another way to caricature people is to draw them ridiculously short and squat. This is a good way to draw bossy people who always tell you what to do — like teachers or scout leaders. It takes away their authority.

Take care with the angles of this shape.

Add two little stick arms.

Two slanting lines mark off her baggy shorts. A short slanting line at the top will form the top of her beret.

Add hands, giving this one a long pointing finger.

Draw in the head, and run a line down the center of the body.

Sketch a comic face, and give her a clipboard to hold.

Draw block-like shapes for the feet.

Make the hair wild and straggly — this woman doesn't worry about her coiffure!

Now draw in her uniform, adding details like breast pockets and badges.

In cartoons, figures of authority always peer over the top of their eyeglasses. The prim little mouth and upturned piggy nose make an entertaining contrast.

Our Girl Scout Leader certainly watches her weight. She has it out in front of her, where she can see it!

Emphasis is laid on the square face and the uniform of huge, baggy shorts and bulging blouse. But the arms, pointing instructions, and solid, sensible legs also work to comic effect.

Soccer Star

Goal! Soccer players don't hide their feelings when they score a goal. Here we capture that moment of celebration. Note how an impression of excitement is given by drawing the figure tilted over at an angle, rather than upright.

A rectangle forms the top of the head.

On either side of your central slanting line, draw these long narrow triangles, like wings. They form the outstretched arms.

Make this triangle the same length as the oblong at the top. It forms the area for the chin and open mouth.

Draw a broad nose on the center line of the face. Divide the lower face with slanting lines, and add large ears to either side.

Below the chest, add a small pair of shorts. Now turn the trailing section of your long slanting line into a leg.

A huge grin dominates the face.

The arms occupy only the lower part of the guideline triangles.

This leg appears only half the length of the other, because it is bent backward, making it look shorter. Speed marks beside the leg help to give an impression of movement.

The goal looks small because it is in the distance, behind the running player. Don't forget to put in the ball — the reason for the player's delight!

Ink in your drawing and color your cartoon soccer star in your favorite team's strip.

Captain: Why didn't you save the ball?

Goalkeeper: What do you think the nets are for?

Chef

An expert at work is impressive — except when he's in a cartoon, when something always seems to go wrong. Cooking a chicken is easy for a chef; but suppose he had to catch the chicken first? 'Stop that bird!'

Seven short lines give you the basis of head, hat, and body. Cartoon chef's always wear the tall white hat that is the mark of their trade.

Three more short straight lines form arms outstretched to grab the bird.

Running legs are easily sketched in with this zig-zag line.

In front of the arms, draw this egg-shape for the chicken's body.

Add detail to the arms and legs. Now you can sketch in the chef's face, using his hat as a guideline to position the nose and ear.

Working outward from the egg-shaped body, draw in the chicken. A round eye, looking backward at its pursuer, and wide-open beak give it a comic look of alarm.

Make sure the chef's hands are lined up with the fleeing bird.

Give the chicken a comb and wattles, feathers on tail and wings — and a trail of feathers behind!

The chef's fingers are spread wide to catch the elusive bird.

His white jacket needs very little extra detail — just add a row of buttons.

'Spin lines' in front of the chef's foot, and long, bold speed lines behind both figures increase the sense of movement.

What do you call someone who's eaten one of the chef's specialties?

An ambulance!

Tourist

Everybody finds the stupid tourist a comic figure. Tourists wear loud shirts they would never wear at home, and usually have cameras glued to their faces. Of course, that's not true when we go on holiday — we are tasteful tourists!

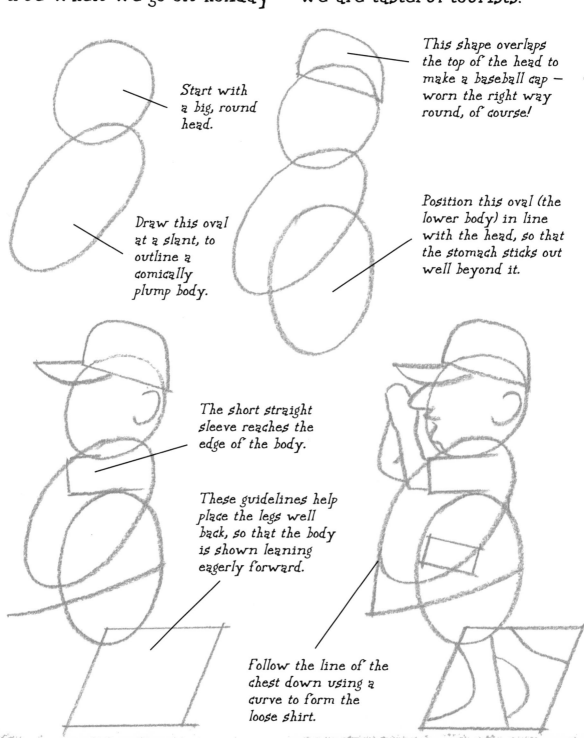

Start with a big, round head.

This shape overlaps the top of the head to make a baseball cap — worn the right way round, of course!

Draw this oval at a slant, to outline a comically plump body.

Position this oval (the lower body) in line with the head, so that the stomach sticks out well beyond it.

The short straight sleeve reaches the edge of the body.

These guidelines help place the legs well back, so that the body is shown leaning eagerly forward.

Follow the line of the chest down using a curve to form the loose shirt.

Fill in the face with chubby cheeks, smile, and sunglasses — and don't forget the video camera!

Use the back of the slanted oval to establish the line that the strap of his camera still follows over his shoulder.

A few simple lines create the sandals.

Smooth out the outlines as you ink them in, so that shoulders and back form chubby curves.

Brightly patterned shirts like this are the uniform of the tourist in cartoons — and often in real life!

Disc Jockey

Another approach to caricature is to link the person's appearance to that of the tools of his trade. Here, the disc jockey is drawn with a big, round head and straight, narrow body. His shape mimics that of the microphone he uses!

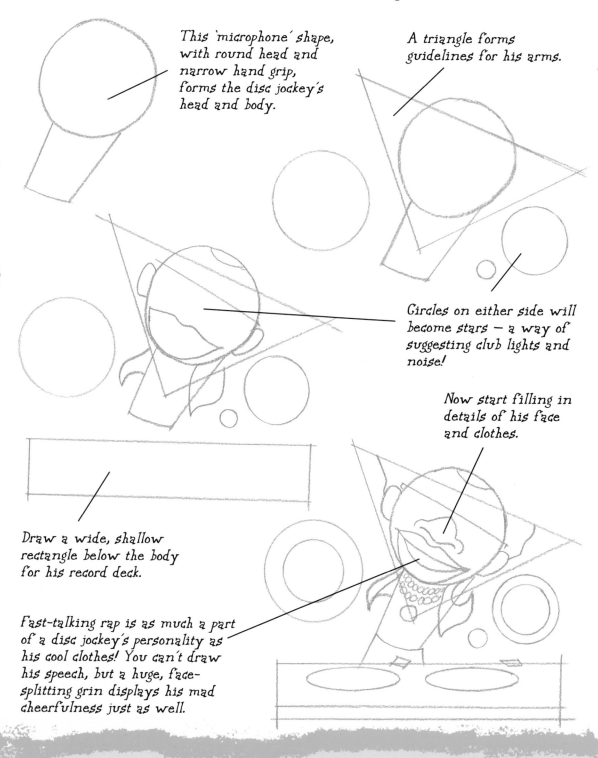

This 'microphone' shape, with round head and narrow hand grip, forms the disc jockey's head and body.

A triangle forms guidelines for his arms.

Circles on either side will become stars — a way of suggesting club lights and noise!

Now start filling in details of his face and clothes.

Draw a wide, shallow rectangle below the body for his record deck.

Fast-talking rap is as much a part of a disc jockey's personality as his cool clothes! You can't draw his speech, but a huge, face-splitting grin displays his mad cheerfulness just as well.

Under a pair of simple eyebrows, draw the outline of large, wraparound dark glasses. These will hide his eyes and reflect the spotlights.

Keep the deck simple. Many DJs have complex, flashy equipment, but you don't want to distract attention from the main man.

Use your triangle to position the short, thin arms, and the hands with their pointing fingers.

Shape the edges of your circles into jagged edges to form stars. Giving one straight edges and the other curved makes a zappy effect.

My father asked if the disc jockey would play requests?

I told him, 'Yes, of course.' He said, 'Then ask him to play chess!'

Butler

The joke about butlers in cartoons (and often in films and books) is that they are usually much grander than their employers. Smart clothes, highly polished shoes, and a snooty expression are essential!

The head is long and tilted back to create a 'nose in the air' expression.

The body and front leg are tilted too, but at a slightly less steep angle than the head. Slanted lines across the trouser bottoms mark the tops of his shoes.

The cover of his serving dish is easily drawn as a half-circle.

Draw a large 'shark-fin' shape for his nose that is held haughtily in the air.

The arm fits neatly within the shape of the body.

Sketch in his jacket, with its long tails.

Finish his trouser bottoms with curving lines, leaving a space above the shoes for his white spats.

Start to fill in the details of his face and add a serving handle to the silver dish.

Start to ink in your cartoon. Just a few well-chosen details can create a very convincing character.

Use curved lines to give a more natural shape to his trousers, and draw in his shoes and white spats.

Ink in your outlines keeping your cartoon smart and stylish — just like the butler himself!

Small 'action' lines will make your cartoon butler look as if he is walking.

'Jeeves, there's a fly in my soup.'

'What's it doing there, sir?'

'Breaststroke, I think!'

Mister Angry

If the next-door neighbor shouts at you for breaking a window, his anger isn't funny. But if he stamps his foot and screams in a temper tantrum, it is. When grown-ups behave like children, it's a cartoonist's dream!

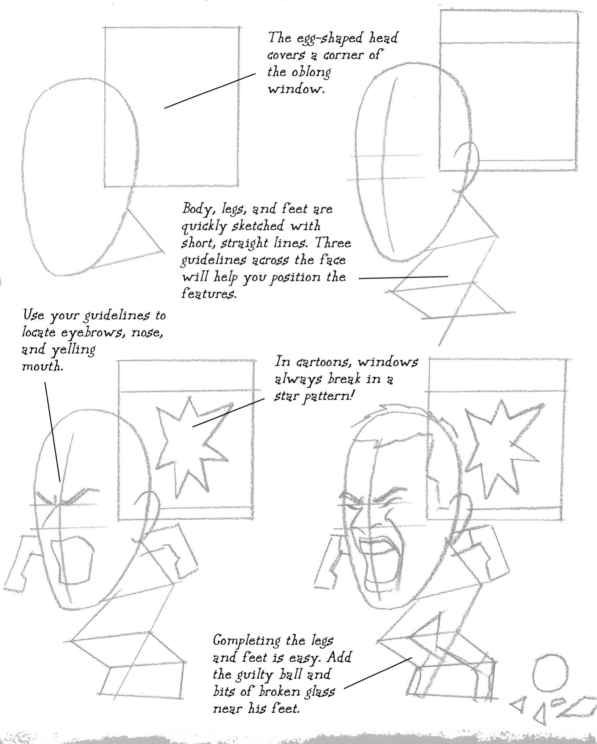

The egg-shaped head covers a corner of the oblong window.

Body, legs, and feet are quickly sketched with short, straight lines. Three guidelines across the face will help you position the features.

Use your guidelines to locate eyebrows, nose, and yelling mouth.

In cartoons, windows always break in a star pattern!

Completing the legs and feet is easy. Add the guilty ball and bits of broken glass near his feet.

CARICATURES

Rugby Player

Cartoons characters are simplified. They usually have either brawn or brains — not both. Rugby players need muscles, so cartoon versions are always big and thick — in both senses! Lack of brains is suggested by a low forehead and heavy, ape-like jaw.

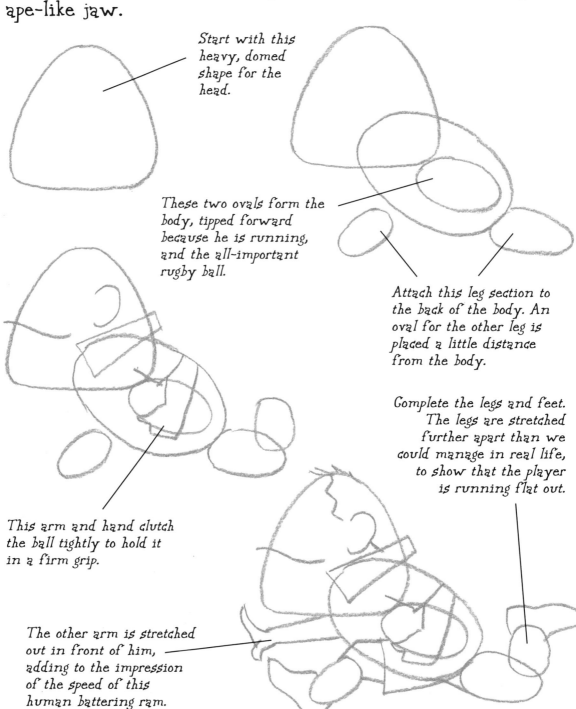

Start with this heavy, domed shape for the head.

These two ovals form the body, tipped forward because he is running, and the all-important rugby ball.

Attach this leg section to the back of the body. An oval for the other leg is placed a little distance from the body.

Complete the legs and feet. The legs are stretched further apart than we could manage in real life, to show that the player is running flat out.

This arm and hand clutch the ball tightly to hold it in a firm grip.

The other arm is stretched out in front of him, adding to the impression of the speed of this human battering ram.

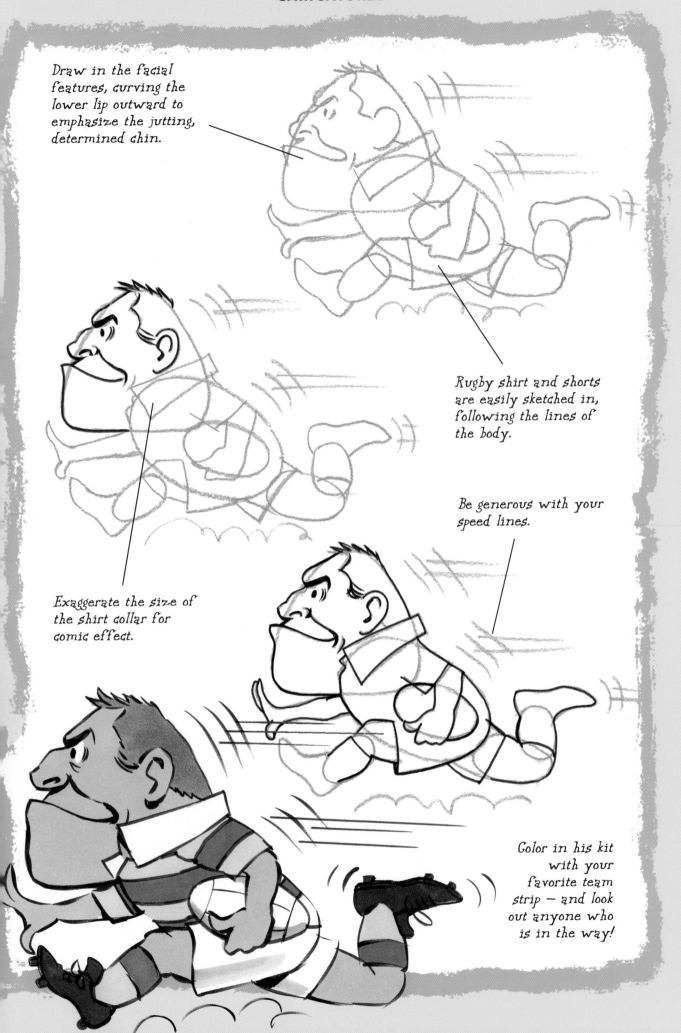

Draw in the facial features, curving the lower lip outward to emphasize the jutting, determined chin.

Rugby shirt and shorts are easily sketched in, following the lines of the body.

Be generous with your speed lines.

Exaggerate the size of the shirt collar for comic effect.

Color in his kit with your favorite team strip — and look out anyone who is in the way!

Policeman

Uniforms help to identify your characters. Cartoon policemen nearly always wear flat hats — because these are recognizable as police uniform in many different countries around the world.

Start with the oval head, and draw a dividing line down the center. Add two horizontal guidelines.

This even-sided diamond will contain the arms and body.

Use your central line to position the nose and a large, sweeping mustache. Add a pair of big ears and add detail to the hat.

Arms and legs are easily drawn following your guidelines.

A disapproving expression is created with small eyes and mouth, both dwarfed by the huge nose and mustache.

Finish drawing the arms and hands, and make the legs end in boots. Add other details like the tie, radio, and nightstick.

Another important detail that helps to identify the policeman are the handcuffs hanging at his belt.

Keeping the face simple allows us to concentrate on the 'What's going on here?' glare. In contrast, the small, neat body in its uniform is drawn in more detail.

Policeman: 'I'm going to have to lock you up for the night.'

Suspect: 'What's the charge?'

Policeman: 'There's no charge, sir. It's all part of the service!'

Horsewoman

You can caricature people by making them look like their interests. Some really do! In cartoons at least, 'horsey' people always resemble their beloved horses. A laughing mouth full of huge teeth is a must, and so of course is a pony-tail!

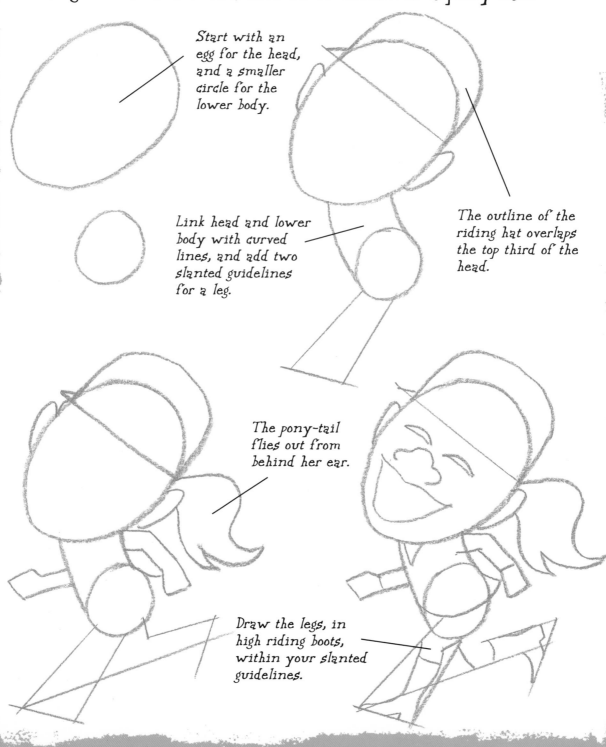

Start with an egg for the head, and a smaller circle for the lower body.

Link head and lower body with curved lines, and add two slanted guidelines for a leg.

The outline of the riding hat overlaps the top third of the head.

The pony-tail flies out from behind her ear.

Draw the legs, in high riding boots, within your slanted guidelines.

Large features fill most of the face. Those teeth look big enough to tackle a nosebag!

People who spend much of their time outdoors often have eyes narrowed from squinting into the sun.

The back of the jacket trails out toward the hand.

A riding crop is the easiest bit of horsey kit to draw!

Riding kit is simple: a smart jacket, jodhpurs, and high boots.

The horsewoman is as active as her pony, moving along at a brisk trot.

Firefighter

Tools can be very tricky things. Even an ordinary hose can tie the user in knots — imagine what a firefighter's equipment can get up to! And, of course, in the world of cartoons things can go much further than in real life!

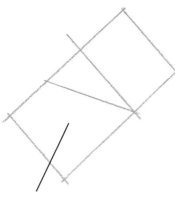

The kicking legs can be drawn as a simple 'V' shape.

Curve the back and base of the body. Cut off the corners of the helmet to give it a more rounded shape, and curve the brim.

Waving arms and outstretched hands show how he is trying to regain his balance.

A slanted oblong doesn't look much like a firefighter's head and body; but just wait. Two lines across it mark out his helmet and arm.

The waterspout spills round him like the petals of a giant flower. Add the jet and the nozzle of the hose at the base.

Finish off his legs with boots. Below the waterspout, draw in a looping line for the hose.

Draw the shocked face and characteristic helmet with its high crest.

Creases in his jacket under his elbow show how his body is bent in two by the force of the water.

Draw in the hose, with a few 'spin' marks to show movement.

His arms and legs flail wildly in different directions.

A few drops of flying water help to make the whole cartoon look even wetter!

Water shoots out of a fire hose at high pressure — maybe it could support a man!

Cricketer

Some funny things happen on the playing field. Here we see what happens when a fast ball meets a slow batsman. Half the fun lies in the cricketer's expression — he doesn't seem to know what has hit him (or rather his bat — and wicket) yet!

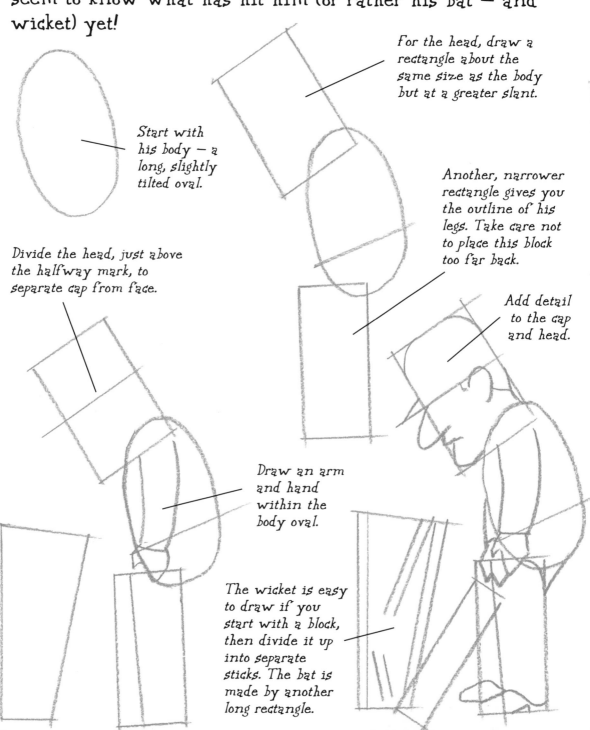

For the head, draw a rectangle about the same size as the body but at a greater slant.

Start with his body — a long, slightly tilted oval.

Another, narrower rectangle gives you the outline of his legs. Take care not to place this block too far back.

Divide the head, just above the halfway mark, to separate cap from face.

Add detail to the cap and head.

Draw an arm and hand within the body oval.

The wicket is easy to draw if you start with a block, then divide it up into separate sticks. The bat is made by another long rectangle.

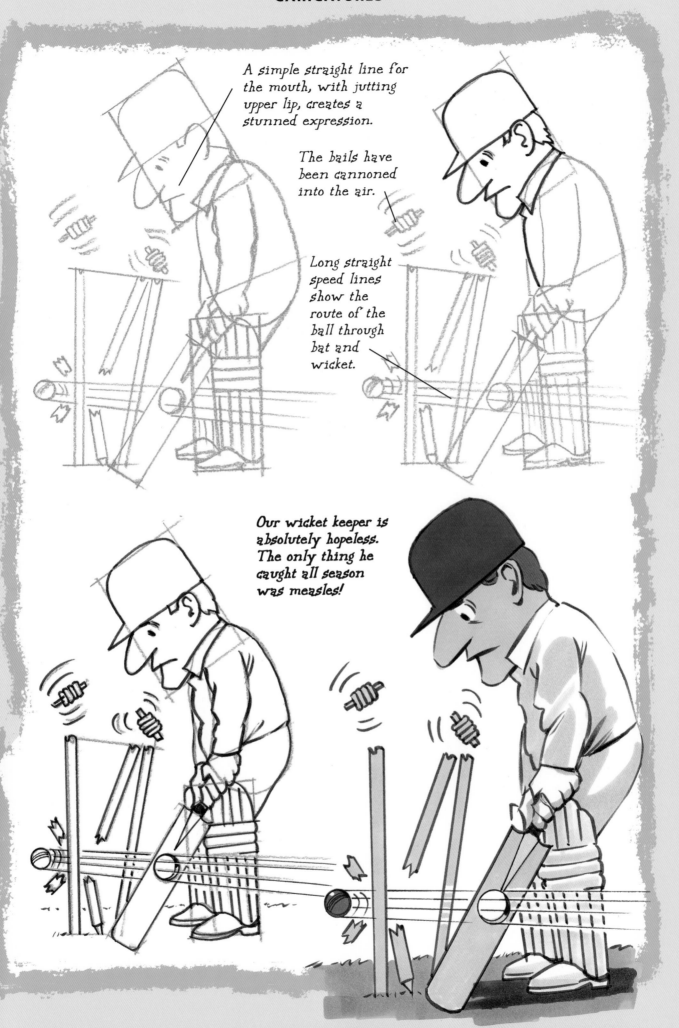

A simple straight line for the mouth, with jutting upper lip, creates a stunned expression.

The bails have been cannoned into the air.

Long straight speed lines show the route of the ball through bat and wicket.

Our wicket keeper is absolutely hopeless. The only thing he caught all season was measles!

Sailor

Some sailors can hit the rocks even on dry land. After an enjoyable voyage, this one is tying up his boat and what happens? A cheeky seagull decides to use his head as a perch! You can have fun with the bird's expression.

Two simple shapes form the sailor's head and body.

Now add a cap and a short, straight arm. Short thin legs make an amusing contrast with the chunky body in baggy shorts.

Add a top to his cap, making it as wide as his head. Give his face a big nose and a protruding pair of ears.

Above the cap, draw the seagull's body and head separately, leaving space for its legs and neck.

A big mustache and tousled hair give our sea-dog a nautical look.

Draw the mooring post, positioning its top just above the bottom of the sailor's shorts.

Finish the face and tufty hair. Make the eyes glare up at the gull. You don't need to draw a mouth — the droopy mustache covers it, and also supplies its expression!

The curve of the gull's beak, and its upturned eye, give it a comically knowing look.

Shape the feet, drawing one sideways on and the other turned toward us.

Draw in the mooring rope, crossing it with slanted lines to give it a twisted look.

A striped T-shirt is standard wear for cartoon sailors. An anchor on the cap badge is also essential!

Why do seagulls fly across the ocean?

They don't want to get their feet wet!

The front of this foot looks wide because it is turned to us. Draw in broad, stubby toes.

Bouncing Baby

A baby isn't just a miniature adult. It's a completely different shape - rounded, with large head, small body, and short limbs. This roundness lends itself well to a cartoon approach — just think circles and you're halfway there!

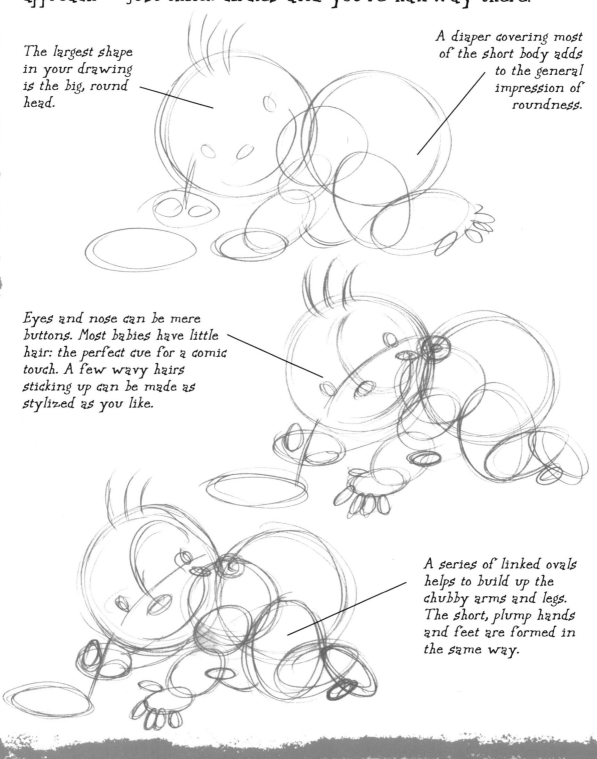

The largest shape in your drawing is the big, round head.

A diaper covering most of the short body adds to the general impression of roundness.

Eyes and nose can be mere buttons. Most babies have little hair: the perfect cue for a comic touch. A few wavy hairs sticking up can be made as stylized as you like.

A series of linked ovals helps to build up the chubby arms and legs. The short, plump hands and feet are formed in the same way.

Draw a little tongue peeping out as a mark of concentration, and add a dimple at the corner of the mouth.

You can suggest the texture of the diaper with little spikes and dashes.

Small children draw very simple faces. The joke here is that the baby's drawing looks very much like his own face.

As you complete your outlines, you can smooth out the links between the ovals of your original sketch.

Babies' toes are more flexible than adults'. Here the big toe is braced against the others for balance.

My little sister entered an art competition.

Did she win?

No, it was a draw.

Jumping Jill

Although actions like jumping feel jerky and sudden, they can be drawn with smooth, flowing curves. This drawing is based on a simple scaffolding of three bold curves. Shapes like head and feet are built up on these lines.

Two ovals form the head and hair.

Start with this framework of flowing lines.

This large foot points downward as she springs up on her toes.

Sketch in the T-shirt as a rough bell shape. Use small ovals to mark out the loose hem, neckline, and armholes.

You don't need to worry about drawing arms and legs with realistic joints. Draw them thin and bendy, like pipecleaners, to suggest freedom of movement.

A curved line across the face helps you to place the eyes.

Keep the face simple with a button nose and smiling mouth. Add a ponytail flowing out behind.

Large hands look less fussy than small fiddly ones.

Rub out the guidelines as you draw in the T-shirt and leggings.

Cartoon characters always have big feet — easier to draw as well as more comical than small ones.

When you have finished erasing your guidelines, most of the original 'scaffolding' lines are hidden. They have done their job in forming a smooth, flowing shape.

Keep clothes simple, so they do not distract attention from the movement. The bold shading produces a lively visual effect.

Baby Driver

A baby seated in a toy car sounds quite a complicated drawing. But you can build it up in stages using easy shapes. By drawing the baby driver as simply as possible, you can focus attention on the toy car.

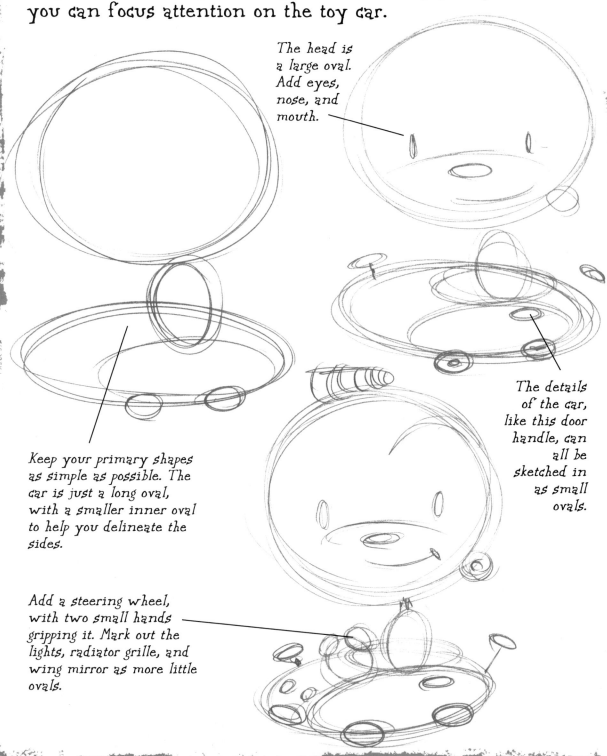

The head is a large oval. Add eyes, nose, and mouth.

The details of the car, like this door handle, can all be sketched in as small ovals.

Keep your primary shapes as simple as possible. The car is just a long oval, with a smaller inner oval to help you delineate the sides.

Add a steering wheel, with two small hands gripping it. Mark out the lights, radiator grille, and wing mirror as more little ovals.

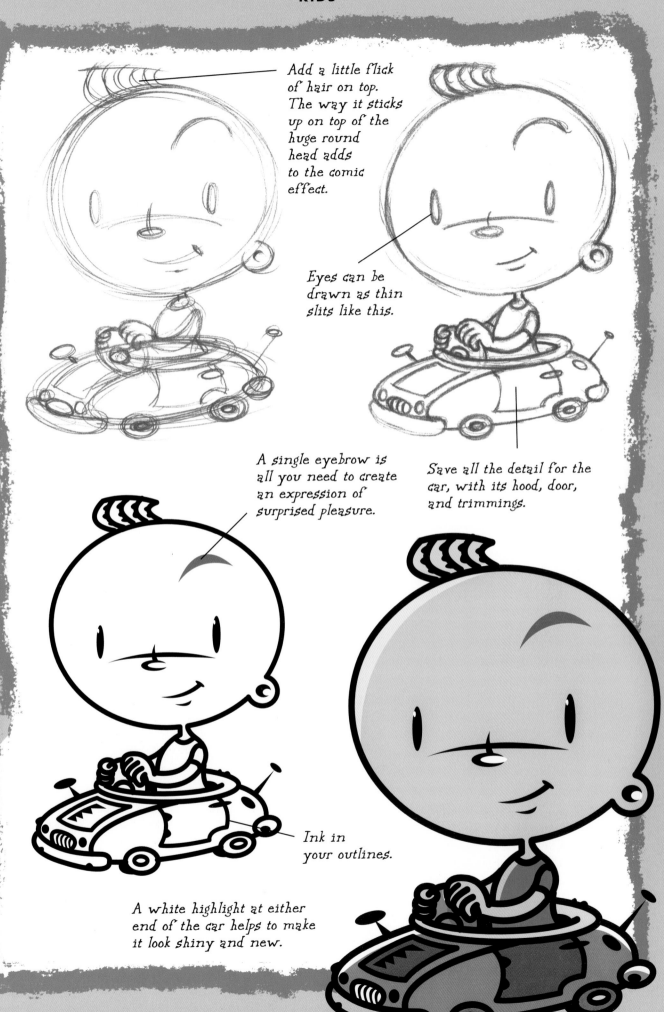

Add a little flick of hair on top. The way it sticks up on top of the huge round head adds to the comic effect.

Eyes can be drawn as thin slits like this.

A single eyebrow is all you need to create an expression of surprised pleasure.

Save all the detail for the car, with its hood, door, and trimmings.

Ink in your outlines.

A white highlight at either end of the car helps to make it look shiny and new.

Happy Harriet

We've all met her — the little girl with too much bounce, always sure everyone is delighted to see her. Now you can draw her! Free, sweeping lines suggest her energy, and we all know what that huge grin means!

A curving line across the head helps you to place the enormous grin.

Use great big blobs for the feet — all the better to bounce on!

Block in the body between the legs, using a couple of ovals to establish the curved hems of jacket and skirt.

Add eyes and nose, and sketch in the grinning mouth. A shock of hair frames the face in a wide, umbrella-like shape.

Outstretched arms rarely stick straight out on either side, except in young children's drawings. By basing the arms on a curved line, you give them a more natural shape.

A collar and three buttons complete the jacket.

One foot is still in mid-air — Harriet is far too bouncy to stop moving while her picture is drawn!

Draw in the wrinkles of socks collapsing toward her ankles.

Even her hair looks energetic as a result of this bold, zig-zag outline.

Draw the top teeth and tongue within the smiling mouth.

Don't forget to add little highlights to add sparkle to the eyes.

Simon the Skateboarder

Scooting along on a skateboard
demands a great sense of balance.
You can't show this in a drawing
just by showing the skateboarder
standing upright. But curving the
body one way and the legs another
captures a sense of dynamism.

*Set the large feet at
different angles on
the board.*

*This large oval will
form the head.*

*Sketch in the
face, setting the
eyes about
halfway down.*

*Make the body short
and distinctly curved
to lean backward.*

*Now you can draw the T-shirt.
Keep the arms and legs curved,
without sharp angles at knees
and ankles, to maintain a
feeling of flowing movement.*

*The skateboard
is easy to draw
— just a large
ellipse with
oval wheels.*

Add a curve behind the head for hair, with an oval on top for the fringe.

This leg looks shorter because it is further away from us — and bent at the knee.

The T-shirt juts out at the back beyond the legs.

Rub out your guidelines and carefully ink in the outlines.

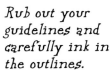

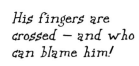

His fingers are crossed — and who can blame him!

Adding shadows beneath his feet makes the board look more solid, while the bold shading on the clothes makes the drawing look really modern.

Snowballing

Clothes are important in cartoons as well as actions. People playing in the snow need to dress up warmly. The bulky clothing sets your scene just as much as the snowball itself.

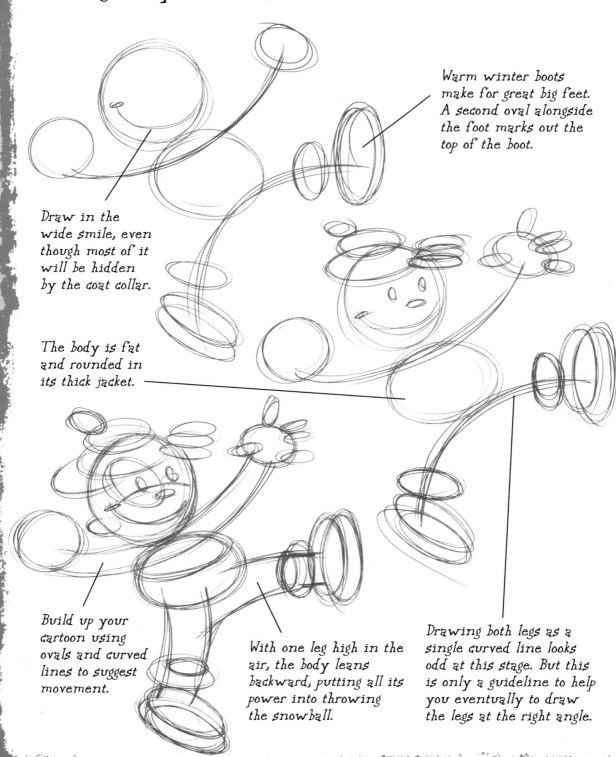

Warm winter boots make for great big feet. A second oval alongside the foot marks out the top of the boot.

Draw in the wide smile, even though most of it will be hidden by the coat collar.

The body is fat and rounded in its thick jacket.

Build up your cartoon using ovals and curved lines to suggest movement.

With one leg high in the air, the body leans backward, putting all its power into throwing the snowball.

Drawing both legs as a single curved line looks odd at this stage. But this is only a guideline to help you eventually to draw the legs at the right angle.

The lower part of this circle becomes a hand, with fingers curved around the snowball.

Only part of the face appears between hat and jacket collar.

Add detail to the jacket and sleeves with a series of ovals to create the padding.

The zigzag line of the jacket zip follows the curves of the jacket. Don't forget the zip tag!

Use bright colors for your snowballer's winter clothes.

There's no business like snow business!

Bouncing Billy

Bouncing on a giant spacehopper is great fun — but how do you get off? The humor in this cartoon lies in the boy's worried expression. It has just occurred to him that he is stuck, and sooner or later he is going to have to take a tumble.

This leg curves over the top of the ball.

The whole drawing is built up of rounded shapes.

Complete the head shape with another interlocking circle.

The lower leg curves roughly across the center of the spacehopper.

Now you can start outlining arms and legs. Remember to use curves rather than straight lines.

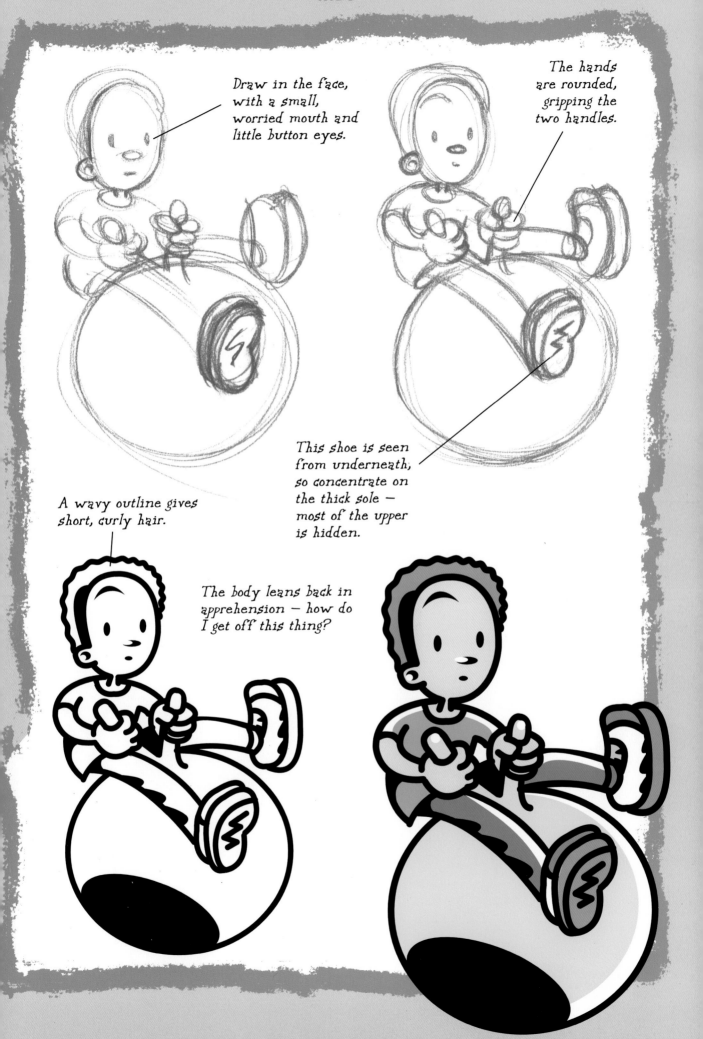

Draw in the face, with a small, worried mouth and little button eyes.

The hands are rounded, gripping the two handles.

This shoe is seen from underneath, so concentrate on the thick sole — most of the upper is hidden.

A wavy outline gives short, curly hair.

The body leans back in apprehension — how do I get off this thing?

Time for Tennis

Tennis is a game that many players take very seriously. Try to draw the effort that goes into following the ball, and the player's total concentration on the action. It's supposed to be fun, but here it looks more like hard work!

Use smooth, flowing curves to suggest movement. Roughly position ovals for the head, hands, feet, and racket.

Nearly all the lines lean the same way, as the player strains to one side to try to hit the ball. His free hand curves the other way to help keep his balance.

This small circle will form the tennis ball.

Strong curves — semi-circles, in fact — shape the bent legs. All the weight of the leaning body is balanced on one foot, while the other swings upward.

The face turns toward the ball, so its features are not central but shifted to one side.

Clean up your guidelines and start to smooth out your outlines.

The ball is coming just over his head, toward the racket.

Suggest the racket strings with a few criss-cross lines.

Hands can be very expressive. Here the fingers and thumb are flung out widely as the player strains toward the ball.

Bob's Balloon

Draw the balloon as a long oval.

Short curved lines form arms, legs, and body.

Here we have Bob, taking his balloon for a walk. Perhaps he is coming home from a party — he certainly looks happy enough. Flying a balloon is a simple pleasure: keep your drawing simple to match.

Make the head a slightly flattened circle.

Hair doesn't have to be realistically drawn — have some fun with it!

A huge beaming smile runs right across his face.

Draw in his pants as wide tubes, with deep cuffs.

Bob's sweater forms a simple bell shape above his legs.

Bob's thumb closes over the string. You've got to hold tight!

A simple patch pocket enlivens his jumper.

The balloon's string ends in a decorative curl.

Add a knot at the end of the balloon.

One foot is flat on the ground, the other raised in mid-step.

Board Rider

This skateboarder is confident that he has mastered all the tricks of his sport. He's leaning with the board on a radical ride, grinning happily. Drawing the board at an angle with flattened wheels gives the impression of speed.

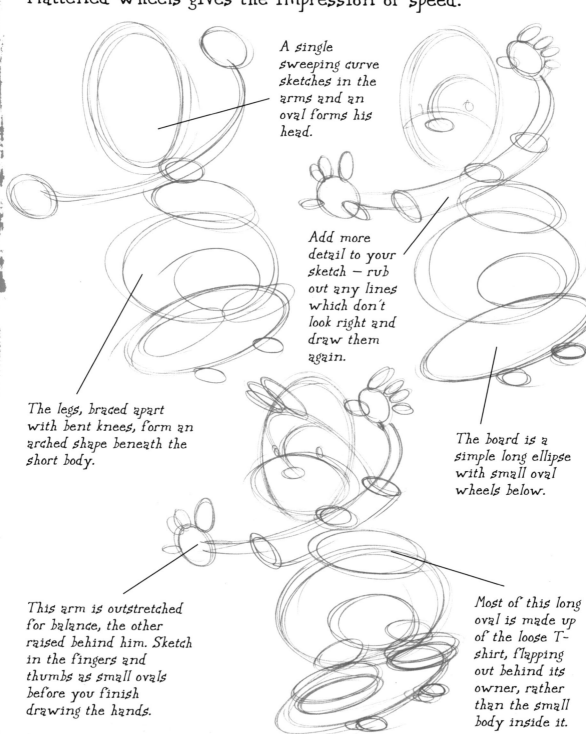

A single sweeping curve sketches in the arms and an oval forms his head.

Add more detail to your sketch — rub out any lines which don't look right and draw them again.

The legs, braced apart with bent knees, form an arched shape beneath the short body.

The board is a simple long ellipse with small oval wheels below.

This arm is outstretched for balance, the other raised behind him. Sketch in the fingers and thumbs as small ovals before you finish drawing the hands.

Most of this long oval is made up of the loose T-shirt, flapping out behind its owner, rather than the small body inside it.

Start drawing in the face in more detail.

Add a wide grin. This is cool!

Draw in the big boots, heels together.

Fill in the body, and the flare of the T-shirt behind.

Clumps of hair fly out through the front of the reversed baseball cap.

Ink in the outline — add solid shadows to give your cartoon more definition.

Draw the skateboard wheels at an angle to show speed.

Most of the guidelines remain as final lines in this drawing — not too much rubbing out! Now you can add bright colors.

Handstand Harry

It's no good drawing someone standing upright, then turning the paper upside down! You need to convey the effort that goes into the exercise. Most people, when doing a handstand, bend their bodies and legs — especially if they're not expert gymnasts.

Draw the feet pointing in different directions.

The body leans over to one side. Draw it loosely using flowing lines.

A shallow oval at the base of the head will help you to form the chin.

Use your curving guidelines to draw in the bent legs.

The egg-shaped head doesn't quite reach the floor — leave room for hair hanging down. Sketch in the curve of the smiling mouth.

Now add the hair, hanging toward the ground and almost filling the space between the arms.

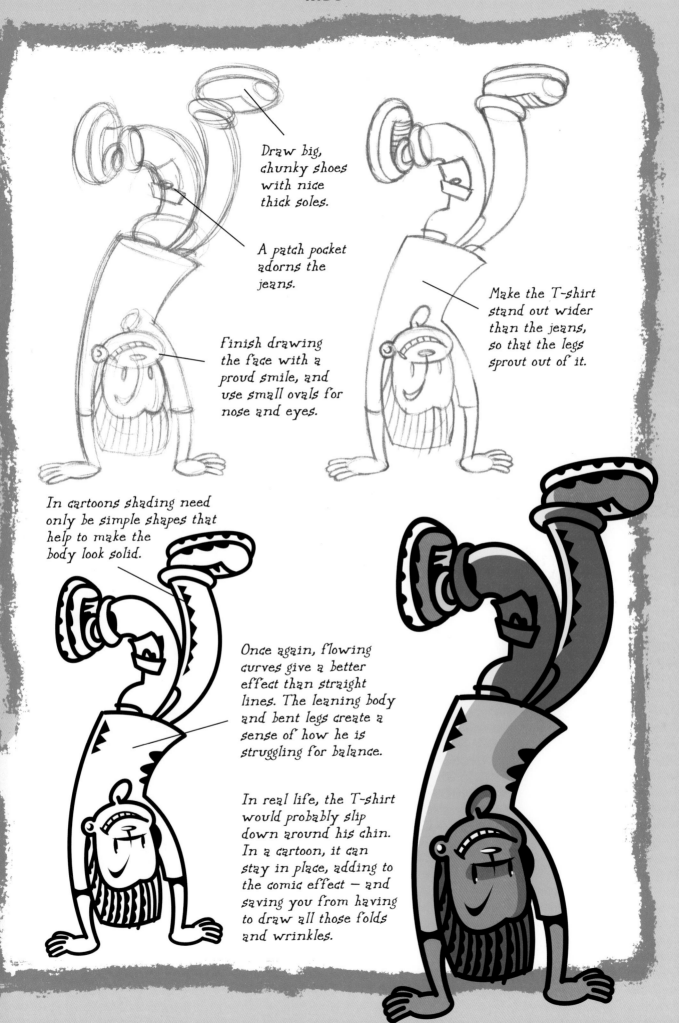

Draw big, chunky shoes with nice thick soles.

A patch pocket adorns the jeans.

Finish drawing the face with a proud smile, and use small ovals for nose and eyes.

Make the T-shirt stand out wider than the jeans, so that the legs sprout out of it.

In cartoons shading need only be simple shapes that help to make the body look solid.

Once again, flowing curves give a better effect than straight lines. The leaning body and bent legs create a sense of how he is struggling for balance.

In real life, the T-shirt would probably slip down around his chin. In a cartoon, it can stay in place, adding to the comic effect — and saving you from having to draw all those folds and wrinkles.

Scooter Sue

Scooters aren't the fastest thing on two wheels. But this rider obviously thinks she's racing along. You can create the impression of speed by making the rider lean back, with her hair streaming behind.

Set the circle for the body just behind the head and legs.

The scooter is easily sketched — base, wheels, and handlebars. Place two big feet firmly on the base.

Sketch in a simple, smiling face.

Link the body circle to the legs with a couple of small ovals, to create a rounded, curved shape.

Sketch in the short, sturdy legs, bent backward to maintain balance. The effect is that the body is being dragged along by the speeding scooter.

Now you can start to draw the face and flyaway hair.

Add detail to the hair — spikey at the front, and streaming out smoothly behind. Don't forget, you can rub out guidelines as your cartoon takes shape.

Use your guidelines to draw in the small wheels. You don't need to attach the front wheel to the scooter — just curve a wheel arch above it.

Make the T-shirt extra wide, so that it streams out behind too.

Now you can ink in your outlines using smooth curving lines. Simple black shapes will create shadows and creases.

Pop, can I have an encyclopedia?

Certainly not, you can walk to school like all the other kids!

Skipping Sam

This good old playground game goes in and out of fashion, but there's always someone with a skipping rope. Skipping can be graceful, but perhaps not with huge trainers and a rope that's starting to collapse!

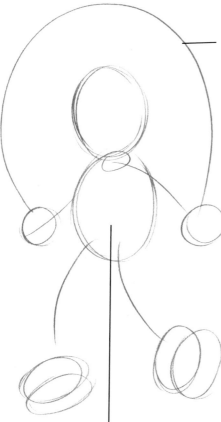

The rope curves high above the figure from hand to hand.

Mark out where the shorts end, halfway down the legs, with small ovals.

Start with a simple figure made up of circles and ovals, linked by curved lines for arms and legs.

Sketching two overlapping ovals for each shoe will help you fit in the thick soles.

Sketch in the baseball cap, hair, and a happy smile.

Add detail to the T-shirt and shorts, bending the body and legs backward to show movement.

Draw in the hands, gripping the rope's handles.

Establish the curve of the rope, and add a couple of kinks to the ends.

Short, skinny legs appear between shorts and sneakers.

Don't skip the task of rubbing out unwanted guidelines! You can make your cartoon as bright as you want.

Soccer Crazy

Soccer players twist themselves into some astonishing positions when trying to reach the ball. You hardly need to exaggerate these at all for a great cartoon. Here we have a player who is falling over backward in the attempt!

Draw a circle for the head. A short curve across the lower third marks out where the face broadens below the eyes.

Sketch in the arms along your guideline, and add a circle for the football just in front of a hand.

Body and leg form a single curve, from which the second leg stretches upward.

Add eyes and nose, and a small oval to mark out the ear.

Don't be afraid of rubbing out guidelines and drawing them again until you start to get the correct shapes.

Draw the hand with outspread fingers and thumb.

Small ovals mark out the legs of his shorts, at about knee level.

When you are happy with your rough sketch, finish drawing the face and arms. Your guidelines show you where the T-shirt ends and the shorts begin.

A lopsided grin can be very expressive. Cartoon faces usually don't look realistic because certain features are exaggerated to make them funny.

Thin, bendy arms without angular joints are flung out for balance.

Socks are more interesting to draw when they are falling down! A couple of curving lines form wrinkles.

What did the TV commentator shout when Dracula took a successful penalty?

'It's a ghoul!'

Unicycle

Riding a unicycle takes a lot of skill, and a good sense of balance. But it's more fun to draw someone whose sense of balance is a little wobbly! It probably isn't a good idea to lean quite this far backward in the saddle!

Set the head well over to the side away from the wheel. Use curved lines and oval shapes to plan your drawing.

Draw in the center of the wheel so that the pedal will fit under the foot.

Sketch in ovals for the feet at the top and side of the wheel.

Check the position of the legs. They start safely enough directly above the wheel, then curve boldly back toward the tilting saddle.

The hair forms a circle, following the curve of the outflung arm and interlocking with the oval of the face.

Making the face broader below the eyes gives a cheeky, monkey-like expression.

Hands can be drawn using simple shapes.

Follow your rough guidelines to draw in the rider's clothes.

Start to form smooth outlines as your cartoon develops.

Draw the back of the saddle peeping out behind the rider.

Add highlights to the eyes, and spiky eyelashes.

Break up the smooth fall of the hair with a few floppy locks.

Clean lines and black shading will bring your cartoon to life.

Riding a unicycle is wheely difficult!

Juggling Jack

Juggling is easiest when you use a set of similar objects. To make it more interesting, this juggler is managing to spin a hoop on his leg at the same time as keeping all the balls in the air.

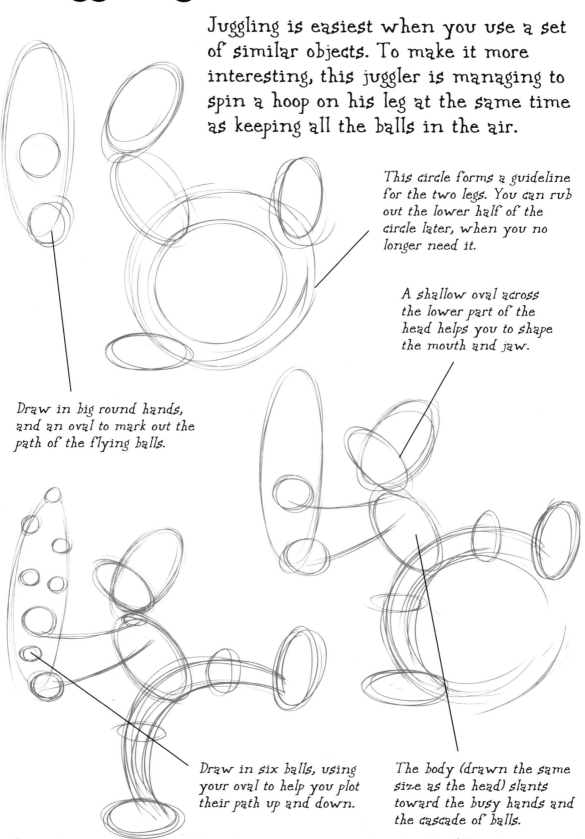

This circle forms a guideline for the two legs. You can rub out the lower half of the circle later, when you no longer need it.

A shallow oval across the lower part of the head helps you to shape the mouth and jaw.

Draw in big round hands, and an oval to mark out the path of the flying balls.

Draw in six balls, using your oval to help you plot their path up and down.

The body (drawn the same size as the head) slants toward the busy hands and the cascade of balls.

A curve around the eyes marks out the position of the eyebrow.

Draw the arms rather long, because they are reaching out to catch the balls.

Use small ovals to sketch in the legs of the shorts, and the tops of the socks.

Position the hoop whirling around the leg. You could add 'spin' marks to show that it is moving.

The hands are slightly curved, with outstretched fingers, to catch and throw over and over again.

Why shouldn't you take a vampire to the circus?

Because he always goes straight for the juggler's vein!

Big, boat-shaped shoes give the juggler a firm base to stand on.

Baby Dinosaur

When we think of dinosaurs, we expect them to be huge and probably fierce. So let's do something quite different! This drawing turns our expectations on their heads by showing a cute baby, who is using his broken eggshell for a cot.

A circle with a slice off the top forms half an eggshell.

Above it, add a slightly slanted egg shape for a head.

Add guidelines for eyes and mouth.

Give the shell a jagged edge, but leave this bit smooth . . .

. . . and draw a pair of claws clinging to the edge.

Add more zig-zag edges behind the claws.

Big eyes and tiny teeth make the hatchling look babyish. You can make him look friendlier by adding speed marks round the tail so it seems to be wagging a puppy-like greeting.

Rub out this guideline when you have finished drawing the claws.

We don't know what dinosaur nests looked like, but sketching in a pile of twigs makes it clear that this egg is in a nest.

Caveman

Cavemen in cartoons always wear animal skins and carry huge stone clubs — it's a 'uniform' by which we recognize them. We don't expect them to look either wimpy or intellectual. You need to be strong to drag a woolly mammoth back home!

A big circle forms the thick body.

Place the short, broad head well down the body.

Long hair flowing outward helps to merge the head shape into the body, giving a bulky, squat look.

Draw the huge clubhead just overlapping the base of the body.

A simple curve forms heavy, frowning eyebrows.

Place the big, round hands about two thirds of the way down the body.

Give the club a tapering handle.

Draw in the face.
Much of the head
shape is taken up
by the shaggy hair
and beard.

Decorate his
garment with
uneven spots to
make it look
like fur.

Give his boots wide tops, and
draw slanting lines across
them for leather ties.

Finish the lower edge of
his garment with a bold
zig-zag edge — cavemen
hadn't invented straight
hems yet!

Tiny crease lines
under the eyes, and
between the eyebrows,
add a great deal to the
expression.

Why is a caveman
never lonely?

Because he always
has his club with him!

Gone Fishing

Hunting and fishing were the caveman's version of going shopping. Of course, it was a bit more dangerous. This cartoon takes a humorous look at one of the risks a prehistoric fisherman might face . . .

Two small interlocking circles start off the figure of the fisherman.

Sketch in the monster's gaping jaws. Add a little oval between the jaws for the small fish, and a blob on the water for the fishing float.

This big sweeping curve forms the monster fish's head.

Thick, bent legs set well apart start turning your two circles into a man.

Finish shaping the man, with his arms stretched forward to hold his rod. A line beneath the figure gives him the shore to stand on.

Give the little fish a tail, and the big fish lips and eyes. In real life, most fish have round eyes, but in cartoons it's more fun to draw a glaring human-shaped eye.

Draw a fishing line from rod to float, and from float to fish.

Finish drawing the caveman. A happy grin appears through his beard because he knows he has a catch — he just doesn't know what he's caught!

Simple jagged lines give the monster fish two rows of giant teeth.

Real fish may not have eyebrows, but cartoon fish have the advantage when it comes to expression. Heavy brows help to make the monster look fierce.

Add a few little bubbles rising from the little fish's mouth.

Rough coloring can be more effective than fiddly work. Leaving a white outline round both fishes makes them stand out more.

Woolly Mammoth

One inspiration for cartoons is having fun with names. We all know that the woolly mammoth gets his name from his shaggy coat. But why not draw him wearing a winter woolly? Back in the Ice Age, he would probably have welcomed it!

Start off with two rough balls — like a snowman.

Shape the hem of the sweater, and add a couple of short, chunky arms.

This arm ends in a curve, like a fin, to give the blunt shape of an elephant-like forefoot.

Sketch in the outlines of a woolly hat to match his sweater.

Draw in the huge, leaf-shaped ears on either side of the head.

The trunk is essential to identify the mammoth.

The tusk fits into a rounded socket.

The eyes are circles with their bases cut off by curves below. These curves help to make the face look chubby rather than flat. The rounded tusk socket helps, too.

A few wavy lines form toenails on the big, rounded feet.

Create a knitted texture for hat and sweater with rows of wiggly lines.

The trouble with knitting a sweater for one of these creatures is that you need a mammoth supply of wool!

Out of the Frying Pan...

The unexpected is always an amusing subject to draw. Here our caveman is running away from a ridiculously huge dinosaur, represented only by its foot. But the cave where he wants to hide isn't quite what he thinks it is!

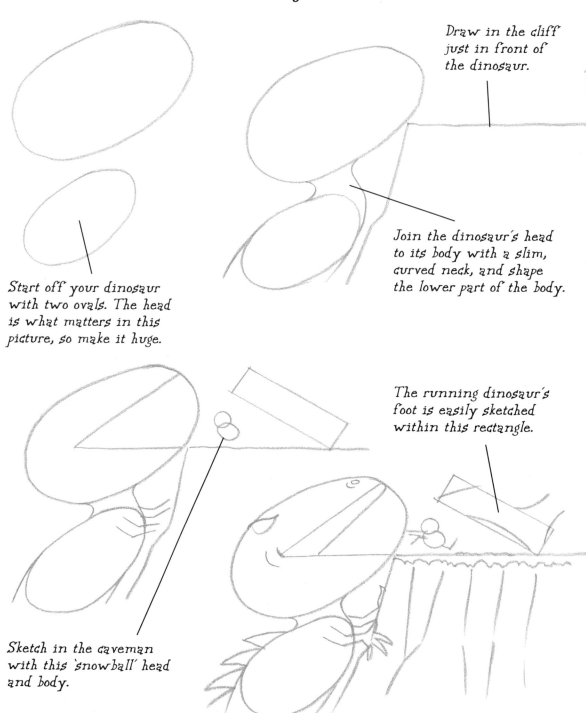

Draw in the cliff just in front of the dinosaur.

Join the dinosaur's head to its body with a slim, curved neck, and shape the lower part of the body.

Start off your dinosaur with two ovals. The head is what matters in this picture, so make it huge.

The running dinosaur's foot is easily sketched within this rectangle.

Sketch in the caveman with this 'snowball' head and body.

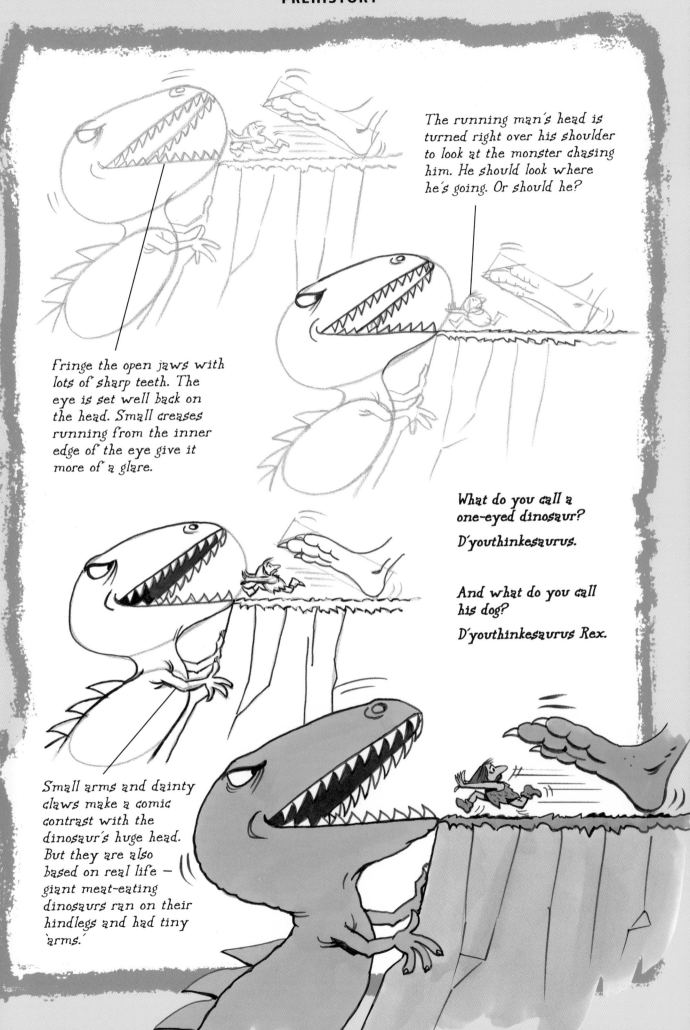

The running man's head is turned right over his shoulder to look at the monster chasing him. He should look where he's going. Or should he?

Fringe the open jaws with lots of sharp teeth. The eye is set well back on the head. Small creases running from the inner edge of the eye give it more of a glare.

What do you call a one-eyed dinosaur?

D'youthinkesaurus.

And what do you call his dog?

D'youthinkesaurus Rex.

Small arms and dainty claws make a comic contrast with the dinosaur's huge head. But they are also based on real life — giant meat-eating dinosaurs ran on their hindlegs and had tiny 'arms.'

Prehistoric Mailman

It's a favorite joke among cartoonists to imagine the Stone Age as being just like ours, but with everything made out of stone. Of course, there would be problems. Imagine having to deliver letters carved on slabs of stone!

This big slab covers most of the mailman's body.

Build up the cart with back, wheel, and a slanted shape for the stack of rocks — I mean letters.

Draw the side of the cart first, on a slight slant. Make sure you set it far enough away from the mailman to leave room for the cart's handle.

Fill in the shape of the mailman clasping his heavy load. His hands are spread out, clutching the stone slab. Add three simple curves on top of his head to form his peaked cap.

Finish drawing the rest of the cart and the stack of stone slabs. Add a small wheel at the front of the cart, and a wooden handle so the mailman can haul it along.

Draw in the wooden framework of the cart.

Screwed-up eyes, puffed-out cheeks, and pursed mouth show the huge effort involved in carrying rocks. Increase this impression with 'spin' marks to show how the postman is wobbling under his load, and sweat drops flying from his face.

Details show how the cart is made, with stone hub caps on the wheels, and criss-cross ties at the wooden joints.

A few rows of short straight lines represent Stone Age handwriting.

Mailman: 'I've had to walk three miles to deliver this letter to your farm.'

Farmer: 'You should have mailed it instead!'

Saber-toothed Tiger

With animal cartoons, ask yourself what is the most obvious feature of your chosen animal. Then imagine what you can do with it. With the Saber-toothed Tiger, obviously it's his teeth. And, of course, he needs to keep them sharp . . .

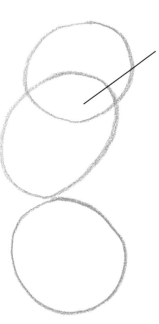

Start with these three shapes — a head and two sections of body.

Two small circles on the head form ears, and a slightly larger one makes a paw. The other paw is set some distance away from and just below the head.

The shield-shaped nose is set high up, because the head is tipped back.

Draw a long shape for the file, running from one paw almost to the other. Leave a space for the handle.

Shape the feet and haunches, and add a curving tail ending in a large tassel.

Draw in the two saber teeth.

Short 'spin' marks show the movement of the file across the edge of the tooth.

Curl the toes of the forepaw round the file handle.

Spiky whiskers show on the left, but are mere dots on the other side of the face.

Make the stripes on the body uneven to match a tiger's markings. The tail is evenly banded, like a snake.

Courting Couple

The cartoon world has its own rules, whereby certain characters always behave in the same way. In this world, dogs always chase cats, fat people are always funny — and cavemen always woo their women with a club, and drag them home by the hair.

The man's head and body are the same size, the body slightly slanted.

Add arms the same length as the body. Sketch in the legs, making them very short and set close to the ground.

Draw his woman's head a little distance away.

Sketch in lines for her legs and upturned feet.

Link her head to his hand with this tapering shape for her hair.

Now you can complete her outline, making her slimmer and lighter than her mate . . .

. . . and finish drawing him. Sketch in his long hair, beard, and mustache.

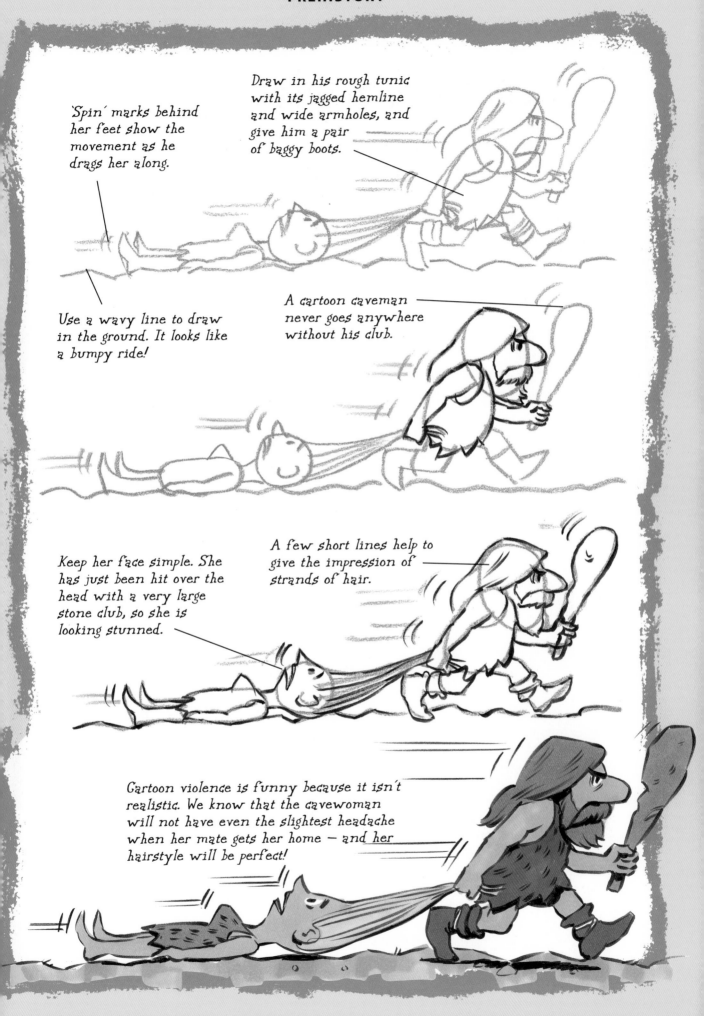

'Spin' marks behind her feet show the movement as he drags her along.

Draw in his rough tunic with its jagged hemline and wide armholes, and give him a pair of baggy boots.

Use a wavy line to draw in the ground. It looks like a bumpy ride!

A cartoon caveman never goes anywhere without his club.

Keep her face simple. She has just been hit over the head with a very large stone club, so she is looking stunned.

A few short lines help to give the impression of strands of hair.

Cartoon violence is funny because it isn't realistic. We know that the cavewoman will not have even the slightest headache when her mate gets her home — and her hairstyle will be perfect!

Pushing the Baby

Simple everyday objects seem comic in the cartoon Stone Age. A baby carriage with massive stone wheels and a leaf canopy is instantly amusing. Silly details, like the baby's toy dinosaur and his mother's handbag, add to the fun.

Start with a long oval, for the canopy.

The body of the carriage is a simple rectangle.

Now add Mom — three blobs form her head and body. Note that the middle blob slants forward to help create a waist.

Draw an uneven line for the ground. Then sketch in the lines of Mom's legs, bending at knees and ankles. Space the legs quite far apart, to show that she is walking briskly.

Add circles for the hub caps of the wheels.

Now you can work on the carriage. Shape the leaf canopy, attaching it to the body with a curving stalk. Add a handle, slanting it across the wheel, and sketch in the baby's waving arms.

Stone Age Mom wears a simple short dress with jagged hem, lumpy boots, and a shaggy hairdo. She is not so very different from a real-life modern mother — as her handbag reminds us.

Curve her fingers around the handlebar.

The baby looks directly at us, beaming and waving his toy dinosaur.

Curved 'spin' marks near the wheels show that the carriage is rolling along.

Cartoon babies have an instantly recognizable 'uniform,' consisting of a big head, a tuft of hair on top, and a single tooth. They are always either crying, with huge open mouths, or smiling widely. This mother is lucky!

Don't forget to show how the primitive baby carriage is held together. Criss-cross lines show where the pieces of wood, and the leaf canopy, are tied in place.

Earthmover

We all know that humans and dinosaurs were not around at the same time. But in the cartoon world, they were! This allows cartoonists to find some unusual uses for dinosaurs.

Two circles form the head and body of the rider (or driver, if you prefer!)

Start with a big square for the dinosaur's head, and an egg-shaped body a little way away.

Use short, straight strokes to sketch in the big jointed legs.

Within your guidelines, create a slanting forehead and massive open jaws.

The tail is as thick as the neck but longer, tapering toward the end.

The driver's face consists mainly of nose and beard.

Give the dinosaur an eye and zig-zag teeth. Then draw in the earth which this living earthmover is shoveling up.

Finish off the feet with rounded toenails, and add little creases at the leg joints.

The driver's seat is a simple structure made of pieces of wood tied together. Use a ruler to mark out its straight lines.

You can see here two different ways that guidelines work. The oval sketched for the dinosaur's body is still recognizable. But the head square is only a frame for the head and jaws, and it will be rubbed out.

Make sure the neck curves smoothly to the shoulders.

In the absence of control buttons, this driver has to work his 'machine' with hand commands.

The driver wears standard caveman 'uniform' of animal-skin tunic and boots.

Nobody knows what color dinosaurs were, so you can choose any color you fancy. You can even copy the colors that your local construction firm uses for its earth-moving machinery if you like!

Doomed Dinosaurs!

Another approach to cartoons is to look at the facts about a subject in a new way. Everyone knows that dinosaurs died out. But let's imagine one of the dinosaurs knew what was going to happen. Would the others have believed him?

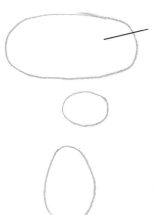

This oval forms the dinosaur's placard. Carefully spaced beneath it, draw smaller ovals for head and body.

Big, fat legs bulge out on either side of the dinosaur's body. Add the stick supporting his placard.

Start the second dinosaur, with an oblong head and oval body.

Continue work on the first dinosaur. Complete his body with a narrow chest, and sketch in wide blocks for his feet. Add a plump, tapering tail.

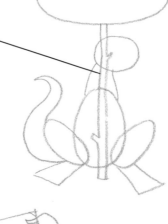

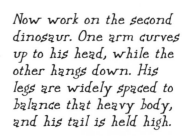

Now work on the second dinosaur. One arm curves up to his head, while the other hangs down. His legs are widely spaced to balance that heavy body, and his tail is held high.

The dinosaurs' expressions are important. The placard holder looks understandably worried, with downcurved eyebrows and mouth.
But the other's brows and mouth slant upward — he's laughing his head off.

But this dinosaur is up on his toes in a bouncy position — he's not worried. He taps his own forehead as if to say, 'You're nuts!'

The first dinosaur's claws curve round his placard stick, clutching it tightly to himself. His whole demeanor looks miserable.

'Spin' marks draw attention to the movement of his hand.

THE END OF THE WORLD IS NIGH!

Late for Work

Things that happen every day in real life make great cartoons when drawn in a different setting. You've seen people hurrying to work in the rush hour. How would a caveman cope with this? He wouldn't have a fast car!

Two rounded shapes form the rider's head and body. Make his body slant slightly, so that he is leaning back in the saddle.

The dinosaur's head and body are long ovals, spaced well apart to allow for the neck.

Turn your two ovals into a man by adding arms and legs. One arm swings forward to hold the reins, while the other swings back to drive his mount on. Below his foot, draw an oval for the top of the dinosaur's leg.

The long, tapering tail curves slightly upward toward the end.

Link the head and body with a long neck, growing wider toward the chest.

The slim legs are at full stretch. Notice how the back foot curves upward as it swings up from the ground.

Give the dinosaur a face, and mark out the noseband of the simple bridle.

Draw in the rider's face.

A whirlwind of speed marks shows that the dinosaur is in top gear. A few puffs of dust behind him add to this impression.

The tiny front legs are tucked up out of the way

Most of his face is hidden by a beard, so the grim expression is created by wide eyes under heavy brows, and a downward droop to the mustache.

Add detail to the rider's clothing — a fur tunic with jagged edge, and big boots.

Don't forget to add more speed marks behind the rider.

The dinosaur's toes aren't drawn in detail — so they look blurred with speed.

Dive Bomber

The inventive cartoonist can put dinosaurs to all sorts of uses. Here we have a pterodactyl standing in for an airplane. Try developing this idea: maybe you could use a long-necked swimming dinosaur as a Stone Age submarine.

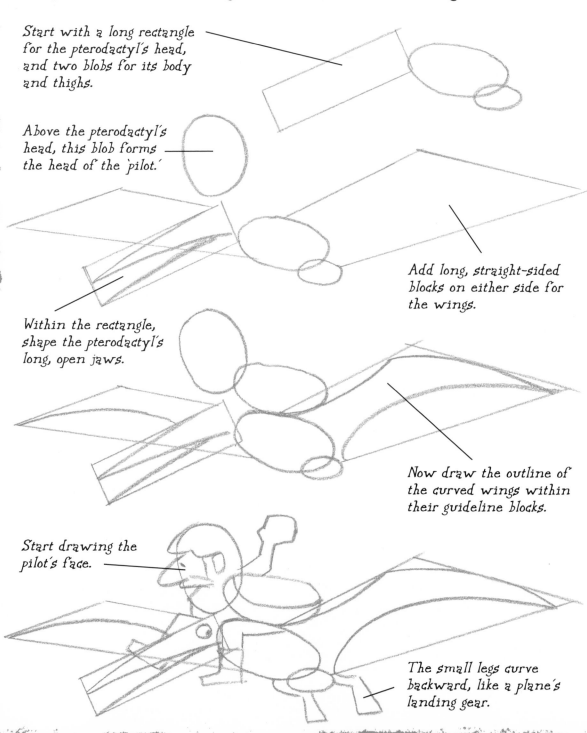

Start with a long rectangle for the pterodactyl's head, and two blobs for its body and thighs.

Above the pterodactyl's head, this blob forms the head of the 'pilot.'

Within the rectangle, shape the pterodactyl's long, open jaws.

Add long, straight-sided blocks on either side for the wings.

Now draw the outline of the curved wings within their guideline blocks.

Start drawing the pilot's face.

The small legs curve backward, like a plane's landing gear.

Add a small curved claw on top of each wing.

Within the outline of the pilot's shoulder bag, draw in his supply of rock 'bombs.'

The pilot's right arm curves forward across the wing.

Start turning the outline of his feet into a pair of boots.

His left hand holds the next stone 'bomb' raised ready to throw.

Roughen the edges of your original oval guideline for the pterodactyl's body. Now it looks like a furry chest, contrasting with the leathery wings.

Near the pterodactyl's head, draw the 'bomb' the pilot has just thrown right-handed, and add speed marks by his right hand to show the movement.

Public Transport

If one man can ride a smallish dinosaur, you can easily get four on a big one. It's simple enough to turn a giant dinosaur into a bus. But perhaps it isn't quite so easy for the Stone Age bus driver to get his vehicle to move!

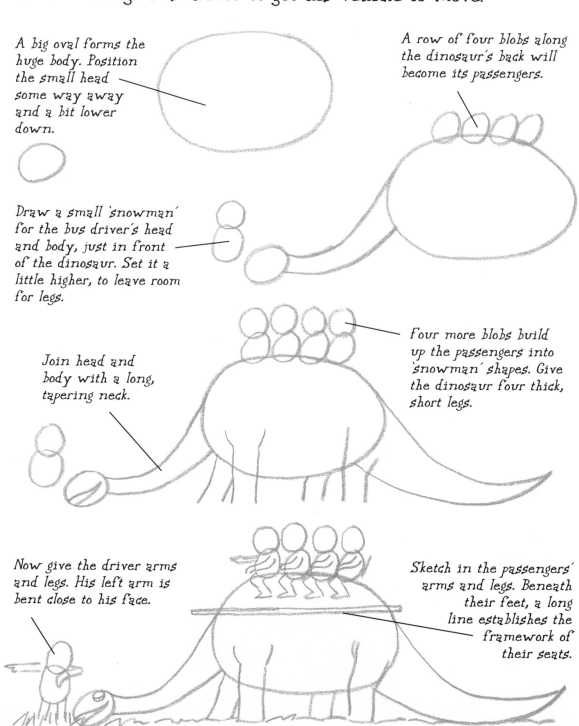

A big oval forms the huge body. Position the small head some way away and a bit lower down.

A row of four blobs along the dinosaur's back will become its passengers.

Draw a small 'snowman' for the bus driver's head and body, just in front of the dinosaur. Set it a little higher, to leave room for legs.

Join head and body with a long, tapering neck.

Four more blobs build up the passengers into 'snowman' shapes. Give the dinosaur four thick, short legs.

Now give the driver arms and legs. His left arm is bent close to his face.

Sketch in the passengers' arms and legs. Beneath their feet, a long line establishes the framework of their seats.

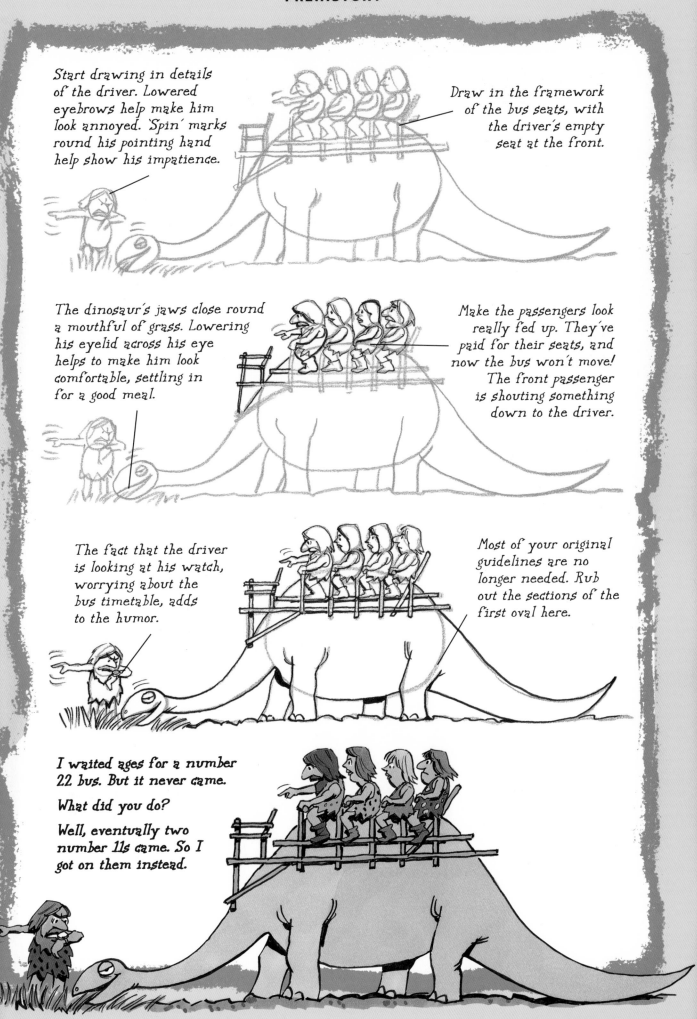

Start drawing in details of the driver. Lowered eyebrows help make him look annoyed. 'Spin' marks round his pointing hand help show his impatience.

Draw in the framework of the bus seats, with the driver's empty seat at the front.

The dinosaur's jaws close round a mouthful of grass. Lowering his eyelid across his eye helps to make him look comfortable, settling in for a good meal.

Make the passengers look really fed up. They've paid for their seats, and now the bus won't move! The front passenger is shouting something down to the driver.

The fact that the driver is looking at his watch, worrying about the bus timetable, adds to the humor.

Most of your original guidelines are no longer needed. Rub out the sections of the first oval here.

I waited ages for a number 22 bus. But it never came.

What did you do?

Well, eventually two number 11s came. So I got on them instead.

Artist

It's easy for you to sit down to draw. You have a table and chair to sit on, and pencils and paper are easy to buy. But what about the Stone Age artist? He had stone to sit on, and stone to paint on, but what did he use for a brush?

Draw the outline of his picture. It isn't quite a square, but slightly slanted.

Add arms. Position this arm carefully across his stone 'canvas.'

Once again, you can start off your human figure with basic 'snowman' blobs.

His rounded rock seat overlaps the base of his body section. Add his bent leg, with the foot just overlapping the seat shape.

A little way away, draw this oval. It doesn't look like a lion's rear end — yet!

Sketch in the easel behind the picture, and draw these ovals for paint pots.

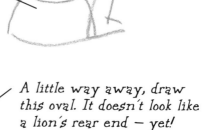

Now draw in the lion's hind legs and long tail, with the all-important 'brush' on the end.

Sketch in the painting that the artist is producing with his unusual brush.

Finish drawing the crude easel — two pieces of wood secured at the top with twine. Make it look thick and solid enough to support a stone 'canvas.'

Complete the paint pots. Make them look chunky, because they are carved out of stone. Cartoon paint pots always have paint spilling messily over the lip. Perhaps yours do too!

You don't need the whole lion to tell the story — just his hindquarters will do.

Draw in the artist's traditional fur garment, giving it a jagged hem and a pattern of spots.

My brother's a terrible artist. He can't even draw the curtains!

Sunday Lunch

Stone Age man lived by hunting animals and gathering plants. What did he hunt? Well, in the cartoon Stone Age he simply has to hunt dinosaurs. The humor in this picture depends on the contrast between the tiny hunter and his huge catch.

Start with a small oval for the dinosaur's head . . .

. . . and a big oval for its body. Leave a good space between the two shapes for the long neck.

This circle, mostly inside the body oval, forms a shoulder joint, with an oval at the rear for a hip joint.

Leaving a good space for the tail, sketch in the hunter as a 'snowman' shape.

Now add the long neck. Make it a big wiggly, so that it looks completely limp.

The thick tail tapers toward the end, where it is tucked over the hunter's shoulder.

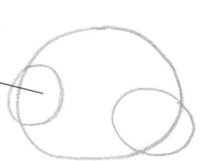

Start shaping the head with a beak-shaped upper jaw.

Because the dinosaur is being dragged along backward, its legs trail at an awkward angle.

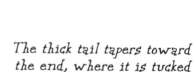

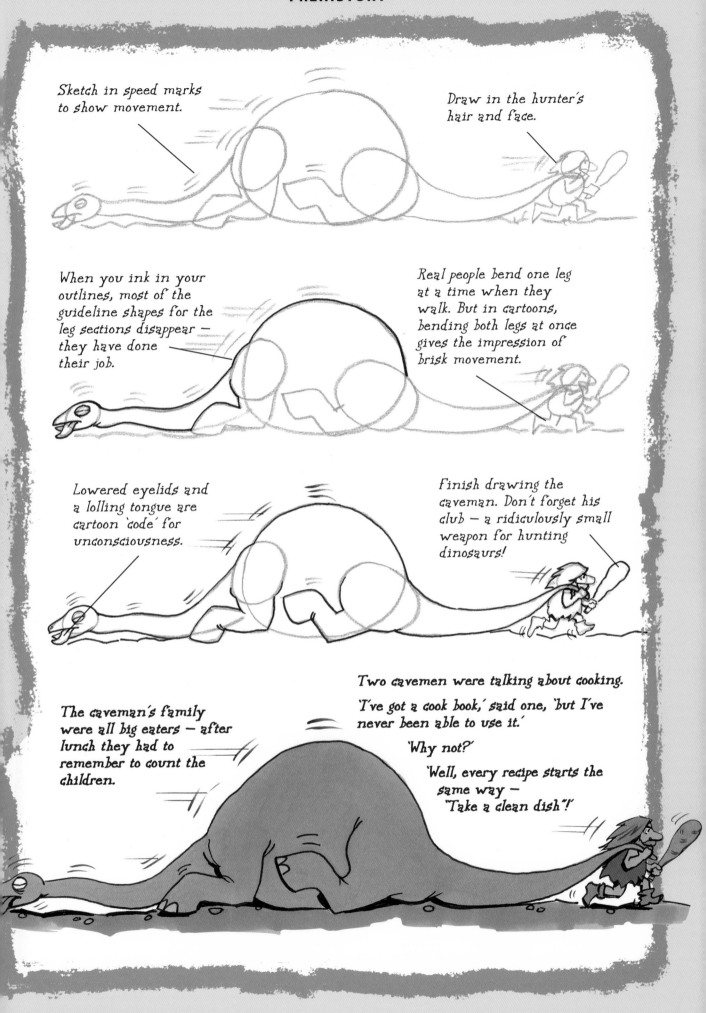

Sketch in speed marks to show movement.

Draw in the hunter's hair and face.

When you ink in your outlines, most of the guideline shapes for the leg sections disappear — they have done their job.

Real people bend one leg at a time when they walk. But in cartoons, bending both legs at once gives the impression of brisk movement.

Lowered eyelids and a lolling tongue are cartoon 'code' for unconsciousness.

Finish drawing the caveman. Don't forget his club — a ridiculously small weapon for hunting dinosaurs!

The caveman's family were all big eaters — after lunch they had to remember to count the children.

Two cavemen were talking about cooking.

'I've got a cook book,' said one, 'but I've never been able to use it.'

'Why not?'

'Well, every recipe starts the same way — "Take a clean dish"!'